Riverside and

the Day

the Bank Broke

Esther Klotz

H. T. Hays, 1903

Riverside and the Day the Bank Broke

A Chronicle of the City
1890 - 1907

by

Esther Klotz

Rubidoux Press
Riverside, California

Cover drawing by Joy Cole
Book design by Vernon Tegland

Printed in the United States of America
Rubidoux Printing Company
Riverside, California

iv

CONTENTS

LIST OF ILLUSTRATIONS

LIST OF ILLUSTRATIONS (Continued)

Preface

Although his name does not appear in the title this is the story of Tom Hays, smooth, dashing, remarkably engaging, a civic leader of immense charisma, who at the turn of the century brought about the failure of the Orange Growers National Bank and created a scandal that rocked the City of Riverside. My purpose has been to recall that period of the city's history when gentility and materialism were so inter-knit that one unscrupulous man could hoodwink an entire community for many years without being discovered.

This book also describes the City of Riverside from 1890 to 1907 when it acquired a new skyline, paved streets, the telephone, electric lights, parks, the automobile, and that astounding new amusement called the motion picture. It also records the early life of Frank A. Miller and the building of his remarkable Glenwood Hotel, which was later to become the world famous Mission Inn.

To my knowledge, except for an excellent two page account by W. W. Robinson in his *Lawyers of Los Angeles* (pp. 128-129), little has been written with any accuracy about Tom Hays.

In 1934 Alfred Cohn, a Los Angeles newspaper reporter, and Joe Chisholm, a lawyer, wrote *Take the Witness*, a biography of Earl Rogers whom they both knew well. Four pages (pp. 141 to 145) describe the Tom Hays case although his name is misspelled throughout as Hayes. The reader derives the impression from this book that Tom was a scape-goat for wealthy men and politicians and was abandoned by them during his prosecution.

In another book, *Final Verdict*, Adela Rogers St. Johns writes of her father Earl Rogers and includes a chapter on Hays. Unfortunately, most of the material about Hays in her book is inaccurate. For instance, she states on page 214 that he never went to jail. *The Riverside Daily Press*, March 24, 1904 records it differently, describing how Tom spent a month and a half in the new Riverside jail. He occupied the then empty women's quarters, while friends sent him cigars, flowers, and liquor.

Strangely, the best account of the rise and fall of this unusual man was told to me in 1965 by Mrs. J. S. Bordwell who lived through much of the excitement. Until her death in 1967 she was a grand old lady of Riverside and the authority on local history. Her home overflowed with books, manuscripts, Indian baskets, and photographs.

In 1880 she came with her parents, Captain and Mrs. Charles T. Rice, to Riverside where they lived near Brockton Avenue on a street now called Rice Road, named for the family. As Anna Rice, her maiden name, she took an early interest in local families and home construction, her father being one of the leading early building contractors of Riverside.

Mrs. Bordwell also identified for me a photograph of a drawing of the Rubidoux Hotel, a building which was never completed. In the fall of 1964 Clarence Swift, Hemet historian, gave me this picture and four other valuable old photographs of the Riverside area which he had rescued from a trash heap. Of these pictures taken in 1887 by "Photographic Artist C. T. Collier," two are reprinted in this work. The photograph of the boom hotel had much to do with the writing of this book. After Mrs. Bordwell related what she knew, I searched the old newspapers over a period of many weeks and slowly put together the story of Rosenthal and the hotel. This was published in the October, 1967 issue of the *Report* of the Riverside Museum Associates. During this search I also began to read about Tom Hays.

Mrs. Bordwell knew Tom well; she even accompanied him occasionally on the piano when he sang at local clubs. I regret that she is not alive to see this book published. I remember her fondly as a friend who always willingly furnished information to someone who wished to write an article, pamphlet, or book on Riverside. Even in the last years of her life she was keenly alert, accurate, and helpful. To Anna Rice Bordwell (1878-1967), who lived at 3987 Crescent Avenue, Riverside, I dedicate this book.

Esther Klotz

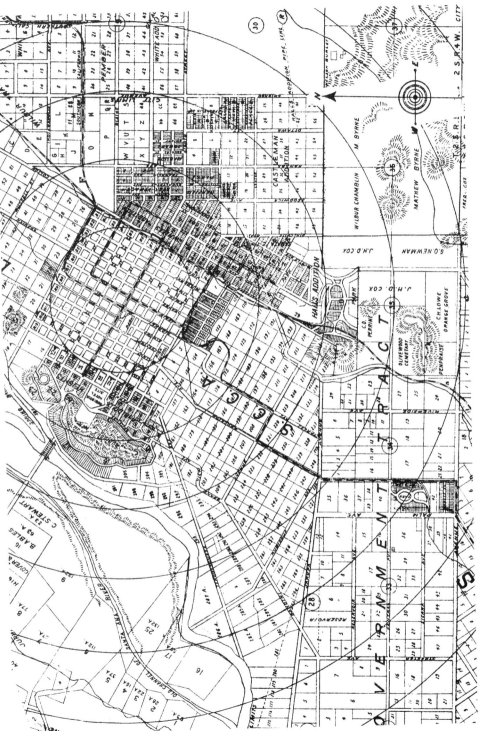

Compiled by A. S. Alkire

Courtesy of Ampelio Luna

President Roosevelt planting the original navel orange tree in front of Glenwood Hotel, May 8, 1903. Wanda Hays, center of picture in white dress.

A. B. BENTON

CHAPTER I

President Roosevelt Comes to Town

On the morning of May 7, 1903 the streets, shops, and hotels of Riverside were elaborately decorated. Palm branches were entwined about the light poles and red, white, and blue streamers hung from the trolley car wires. Gay flags fluttered from the business buildings whose shop windows featured special displays. President Theodore Roosevelt and his party were arriving by train that evening. He was on a western political tour starting his active campaign for reelection in 1904. There were many one night stops on this trip and Riverside was one of those chosen.

This city of about 9,000 people lay on the east bank of the Santa Ana River 60 miles east of Los Angeles. Founded in 1870 as an agricultural colony, it was now well known for its citrus industry and for the Glenwood Hotel which later after further additions would become famous as the Mission Inn. This hotel, managed and recently rebuilt by Frank A. Miller, would house the president and his retinue on their overnight stop. Captain Charles T. Rice and the local National Guard would be in charge of the parade and the security of this important guest.

The Glenwood began as a hotel in 1878 when the Christopher Columbus Miller family first took in paying guests. In 1880 Miller, who wished to continue his work as surveyor, sold the hotel to his son Frank who enlarged it and made it famous for comfort and hospitality.

Early in 1894 Frank Miller incorporated the Glenwood Hotel Company with nine local directors and $250,000 in capital stock. Plans were to move the two wooden barrack-shaped buildings to the rear, remodel the old Miller adobe home, and build a new three story, 160 bedroom hotel on the same site.

In June of that year Miller made a trip to Colorado to inspect its fine resort hotels. In his opinion Walter Raymond's Hotel Colorado built in 1893 at Glenwood Springs outshone all the others in elegance and architectural design. Miller, returning to Riverside with the Colorado Hotel plans, determined to build a similar structure with two wings forming an attractive courtyard.

Not until 1902 was he able to secure the capital and build his hotel. When finished in January, 1903 the new Glenwood Hotel had cost $150,000 but the original architectural design had been greatly altered. Los Angeles architect Arthur Benton had drawn the plans but during the construction a Spanish tower was placed at the corner of Main and Seventh street and flaring mission-style arches added to the roof line. Inside, open timbered ceilings and rough brick fireplaces carried out the early California design of the new structure which was widely advertised as the Glenwood, California's Mission Hotel.

The honor of entertaining the President of the United States would add much to the hotel's fame. Japanese lanterns hung in the pepper trees around the entire block and a large flag and the presidential portrait framed with flowers stood on each side of the hotel's entrance. Colorful flags of all countries hung from the windows, while inside, roses decorated the lobby and tables in the large dining room. At the west end where the president would dine in the evening hung a large bell covered with white roses.[1]

While the hotel was under construction in 1902 Tom Hays, cashier of the Orange Growers Bank and an important man about town, arranged with Frank Miller for the occupancy of the hotel's best suite of rooms. When they were finished Hays, his wife, and 12 year old daughter moved into four rooms on the main floor of the southeast wing. These rooms furnished with Turkish rugs and Chinese furniture seemed the most suitable for President Roosevelt during his one night stay. A few days before the president's arrival the Hays family moved to other rooms so that the suite could be suitably prepared. Florist Franz Hosp and the women of the hotel did the decorating, carrying out the motif of the vigorous, athletic life of Mr. Roosevelt. Boxing gloves, fencing foils,

---

1. *Riverside Daily Press*, May 8, 1903.

and firearms were placed among roses, pine boughs, and oranges and on the wall an elk's head peered through spruce branches. A fern canopy hung over the antique Napoleonic bed which Tom had found and installed especially for the use of the president.[2]

Early in the day trains brought visitors to Riverside from all over the county, and carriages, wagons, and bicycles kept adding people to the busy streets. In the afternoon a big crowd watched the laying of the cornerstone to start construction of the new $145,000 Riverside County Courthouse on Main Street between Tenth and Eleventh. Riverside's Military Band in blue and white uniforms and Company M, the local National Guard, assisted the Grand Order of Masons with the impressive ceremonies.

On schedule at ten minutes past six in the evening, President Roosevelt and staff, accompanied by California's Governor G. C. Pardee, Benjamin Ide Wheeler, Nicholas Murray Butler, and "Teddy's Terrors" arrived by train at the Pachappa Station on Jane Street. The welcoming committee, which included Mayor C. L. McFarland, Senator M. J. Daniels, George Frost, and E. A. Chase, greeted the presidential party and then all climbed into the 11 gaily decorated carriages. The president's carriage was covered with pink and pale yellow roses and the top, which was thrown back, was entwined with pink flowers. The large bay horses were thickly collared with a mass of yellow and pink blooms. Under the leadership of Mrs. L. F. Darling the ladies of the Riverside Woman's Club had worked hard all day and everyone agreed that their work was highly artistic. The presidential party drove on Jane Street to Victoria Avenue and through the C. E. Rumsey orange groves where the group stopped to taste the tree-ripened fruit. From there they went to the William Irving place and on to the head of Victoria Avenue near Victoria Hill. Here the president assisted in planting a 55 foot *Washingtonia robusta* palm tree dedicated to Queen Victoria but later called the Roosevelt Palm. C. E. Rumsey had given the palm tree which had been moved from the Hendry place on North Orange Street to the new location.[3]

After the tree planting all drove into town where a crowd met them at Lime and Fourteenth streets and paraded to a decorated speakers' platform erected in front of the Hayt Building at Seventh and Main. As it grew dark the many red, white, and blue overhead lights added to the colorful scene. Here the president spoke on the beauty and prosperity of Riverside, the benefits of irrigation, the right kind of citizenship,

2. *Riverside Enterprise*, May 8, 1903.
3. *Riverside Daily Press*, May 7, 1903.

Courtesy Roy L. Haglund.

Apartments of H. T. Hays, in the New Glenwood, California's Mission Hotel at Riverside, California, where President Roosevelt remained during his visit to that city May 7 and 8, 1903.

and the attractive Riverside children.[4] By the time the speeches ended, it was dark and the elite of Riverside hurried to join the presidential party at the 44-dish banquet in the Glenwood.

This dinner, one of the finest ever served in Riverside, began with caviar on toast, followed by consomme alphabets or chicken broth au riz, which were served with side dishes of salted walnuts, India relish, chow chow, and plain lettuce. The fish course included boiled salmon-hollandaise with sliced cucumbers, fried halibut with tartar sauce, and potatoes Parisienne.

The main entrees were boiled leg of lamb with caper sauce, braised small tenderloin a la ravigote, creamed sweetbreads in cases, pineapple fritters, glace au kirsch, prime ribs of beef with pan gravy, and stuffed young turkey with cranberry sauce. Vegetables included mashed potatoes, asparagus, green peas, string beans, steamed new potatoes, boiled rice, and lobster salad.

Desserts offered were homemade apple and mince pies, vanilla ice cream, lemon jelly, panoche, chocolate cake, lady fingers, kisses, macaroons, and fruit. American, Swiss, Imperial, and Edam cheeses were served with hard water crackers, salted chips, nuts, pressed figs, dates, and clusters of raisins. The newspaper reporting the menu called it a cold water banquet as no wine appeared on the tables. Beverages included Ramona punch, coffee, and ice water; Roosevelt was a prohibitionist.[5]

The 400 people who attended never forgot the occasion, especially those who shared the presidential table. These included city officers, important Republican officials, and members of the Executive Committee for Arrangements. Tom Hays as a member of this committee and as Chairman of the Riverside County Republican Committee sat with the president.[6]

All night, while the president slept in his Napoleonic bed, Riverside's Company M in full escort duty uniforms and wearing swords, capes, and white gloves, carefully guarded the entire hotel. At 8 o'clock the next morning the president and his party left Riverside for Ontario and Los Angeles on their special train. Before leaving he assisted in a flag raising ceremony with the Miller, Richardson, and Hays families and in replanting in the hotel's courtyard one of the two famous parent Washington navel orange trees which had been sent to Luther and Liza Tibbets in 1873. Unfortunately this tree died in 1922 and Frank Miller had it cut up for souvenirs, but the other Washington navel tree and the Theodore Roosevelt palm still live.

---

4. *Ibid.*
5. *Ibid,* May 8, 1903.
6. *Ibid.*

The president's visit was a wonderful success and the newspaper took much pride in relating the details. One detail, however, was not printed but soon became an amusing bit of gossip for everyone about the hotel. In the evening when President Roosevelt, accompanied by his bodyguards, entered his decorated private rooms the lights suddenly went out. Fearing that an assassin might be in the room, Roosevelt threw himself flat on the floor expecting an attack. When the lights flashed on after the short electrical failure they revealed all Roosevelt's bodyguards sitting on him with their pistols drawn and pointed.[7]

As for Tom, this event marked the peak of his social and political career. Perhaps, as he sat eating the elaborate dinner with the president, he recalled how he, unknown and almost broke, came to Riverside 13 years previously. From a small bookkeeping job at the Dyer Bank he had come a long way to manage the city's biggest bank, own important real estate and oil property, and become the political boss of the county. Tall, goodlooking, with dark eyes, short mustache and sideburns, he impressed everyone with his graciousness and warm, friendly manner. No one was more charming or better liked in Riverside than Tom Hays.

---

7. Information Gaylor Field, Mission Inn Building, 1972.

CHAPTER II

Tom Arrives in Riverside

Tom Hays, although only 36 years old when he welcomed the president, had become a leader in Riverside city and county affairs. In the summer of 1890, because of a throat illness, he had left his home and job in Lancaster, Pennsylvania, where he had worked for five years as an accountant with the Fulton National Bank.[1] Hays and his wife arrived in Los Angeles to visit his old high school professor Reverend Lowell Rogers and son Earl, who was then working as a newspaper reporter and getting to know the local lawyers. Tom soon learned that bank jobs were hard to find, as Los Angeles still suffered from the financial collapse following the 1887 boom. Before long he went to Riverside, a city that had suffered less during the business decline.

On a July morning of 1890 he walked into the Riverside Banking Company looking for work. His tall, well-dressed figure and air of confidence made the two bookkeepers, M. J. Twogood and George Bittinger think he was a capitalist. Giving his whole name, Howard Thomas Hays, he asked to see bank manager Otis T. Dyer. A little later Tom was introduced as the new bookkeeper. He immediately went to work rapidly packaging coins in paper. The operation was slick and smooth and the older bookkeepers could only stare. They were especially surprised to

---

1. *Riverside Daily Press*, Jan. 12, 1907.

see how quickly he had acquired that $100-a-month job.[2]

Riverside, where Tom had thus found work, was an attractive city in 1890. Most of its 4,683 inhabitants were farmers and shopkeepers. Founded in 1870 by the Southern California Colony Association under the leadership of Judge John W. North, the town had grown slowly until the rapid development during the boom of the eighties. Previously, small brick and wooden buildings stood interspersed with citrus groves, water

Bordwell Photo   *Dyer Brothers' Bank, Riverside's First Bank*

tanks, and windmills. Canal water from the nearby Santa Ana River flowed through the town in open ditches which lined the unpaved streets, some of which were planted to pepper trees by the original colonists. These streets, hot and dusty in summer, were a sea of mud when it rained.

By 1890 a new domestic water system replaced the water tanks and windmills. More trees, some electric lights, and horse-drawn trolley cars had been added to the streets. Many new homes and business blocks, built since the 1887 boom, gave the city a new skyline. The city advertised that it had five hotels, three banks, three large livery stables, two newspapers (the *Riverside Daily Press* and the *Phoenix*), twelve churches, a cold storage and ice works, and ten citrus packinghouses. Much of the city's growth had been dependent upon the profit from the navel orange industry.[3]

2. *Ibid.*
3. *Pen Pictures from the Garden of the World.* (Chicago, 1890)

In the fall of 1889 the city packed its most important citrus crop; it was the largest shipment for that year of any town in southern California.[4] Many raisins were also processed, some from large vineyards like the 70 acres owned by S. C. Evans. There were also large citrus orchards. H. B. Everest owned 100 acres on Magnolia between Jackson and Van Buren and there in his own packinghouse he handled his fruit. To communicate directly with his Arlington Hotel he in 1890 had the Electric Supply Company of Los Angeles install a telephone at his ranch.[5] This may have been Riverside's first telephone, for not until May 12, 1891 did the Sunset Telephone Company run a line from Los Angeles to San Bernardino and on to Riverside to establish a system.

Local Indians, still living in native huts near little Mt. Rubidoux and in the Arlington area near the river, worked as agricultural laborers. Other Indians with long untrimmed hair came from Yuma to pick the grapes. A small early settlement just north of Riverside called Spanishtown supplied other workers who usually preferred tending their own neat little farms and who enjoyed cock fighting and running their fast horses, traditions that stemmed from the days of the Spanish ranchos.

Throughout the city were some Negro families whose children, unlike the Indians, attended the local schools. On May 7, 1890 the African Baptist Church with its 35 Negro members organized. In June other Negroes began construction of their Methodist Church at Howard and Thirteenth streets.[6]

The Chinese, who had the largest labor force, lived in homes as domestic servants or in Chinatown in the Tequesquite Arroyo. They grew vegetables and peddled them in carts, did the town's laundry, and worked in the restaurants.

The city's three banks were the First National Bank, its affiliate the Riverside Savings Bank and Trust Company, and the Riverside Banking Company, where Tom now worked. O. T. Dyer, the founder, came from Illinois with his family and his two sisters. His brother, William H. Dyer of Troy, New York aided him financially in the founding of the bank. At a cost of $1,300 a small, one-storied, white, wooden bank building was constructed near the northwest corner of Main and Ninth streets by the local contractor, A. W. Boggs.[7] A 7,500 pound bank vault was installed after a difficult trip from Colton. The wagon on which it was hauled had broken down and the vault lay in the mud for two days.

The bank, named the Dyer Brothers' Bank, opened for business December 6, 1880 with $30,000 capital. As Riverside's first and only

4. *Riverside Daily Press*, Oct. 26, 1889.
5. *Ibid*, June 29, 1890.
6. *Ibid*, June 19, 1890.
7. *Riverside Press and Horticulturist*, Sept. 11, 1880.

Riverside Banking Company

Photo gift of Clarence Swift

bank it grew rapidly and in 1884 became a state bank renamed the Riverside Banking Company. A year later the small wooden building was removed and construction of a brick building of two floors, complete with its own water tank and windmill pump at the rear, was built at the same location.

In 1890 when Tom arrived the building had been altered with new facing, steps, and pillars, all of marble from the Colton Marble and Lime Company which was managed by L. L. Dyer, another brother of Otis. The bank's capital had increased to $200,000, the largest of any bank in San Bernardino County which then included the city of Riverside. Officers were: Aberdeen Keith, president; Dr. J. A. Brenneman, vice-president; O. T. Dyer, manager; Miss E. C. Dyer (sister of Otis), cashier; and J. H. Goodhue, assistant cashier. Directors included the officers, Dr. C. J. Gill, and Orrin Backus.[8]

During the 1887 real estate boom the bank had made loans to the Gage Canal Company, the Colton Marble and Lime Company, many real estate developments, and to the California Motor Road, which since 1888 had run between Riverside and San Bernardino. Otis Dyer had also personally borrowed money in 1888 from his bank to enlarge his home located on Main Street south of Eleventh. He privately invested in local real estate, in the Bank of San Bernardino, and in the Terracina Land and Water Company. One of the Riverside Banking Company's biggest real estate interests was the Mt. Rubidoux Hotel Association which was then building a $250,000 hotel on the east slope of Mt. Rubidoux.

This development resulted from a plan submitted in January, 1887 to the Riverside Land Company by Emil Rosenthal. The company, owned half by the Riverside Water Company and half by S. C. Evans and his Riverside Land and Irrigation Company possessed land north and west of town including all of Mt. Rubidoux, an area without water. Rosenthal proposed to bring to Riverside a domestic water system which would enable him to irrigate also these lands if he could buy 250 acres for $25,000. When the Riverside Land Company accepted his plan, Rosenthal formed two companies, one to subdivide the property, the other to build a hotel.[9]

Emil Rosenthal came to Riverside in 1872 with his partner, Walter Lyon, who was a relative of the well-known Harris Newmark, a Los Angeles merchant who later wrote the book, *Sixty Years in Southern California*. Previously Rosenthal and Lyon had owned and managed a general merchandise store in Colton. They opened a similar store in

---

8. *Pen Pictures from the Garden of the World*. (Chicago, 1890), p. 467.
9. *Riverside Daily Press*, April 9, 1887.

Photo gift of Clarence Swift   *Architects Design for the Rubidoux Hotel*

Riverside on the east side of Main Street and in 1875 built a larger brick store across the street. At this time Rosenthal was aged 30 and Lyon only 21.

That same year Rosenthal married Anna Unruh at the ranch house of E. J. (Lucky) Baldwin in Santa Anita. Baldwin, a very wealthy land and mining speculator, was then married to Emma, sister of Anna Unruh and was a friend of their brother, Hiram A. Unruh. Hiram later managed Baldwin's estate and was his executor. The Unruh family, of Pennsylvania Dutch ancestry, grew up in LaPorte, Indiana, where the children received a good education. There Anna taught school for three years before leaving for California in 1874 with her sister and two brothers, Hiram and Will.[10]

In 1882 Rosenthal bought ten acres of land at the foot of Mt. Rubidoux between Pine, Eleventh, Pepper (now Redwood) and Eighth streets and built a small house for his wife and their three little children. The rest of his land he planted to citrus.[11] That same year Walter Lyon died

---

10. *Pen Pictures from the Garden of the World.* (Chicago, 1890).
11. *Riverside Daily Press*, Mar. 25, 1882.

Emil Rosenthal   *O. T. Dyer*

and until 1886 Rosenthal ran the store with the help of George Frost.

That year Rosenthal sold his shop to Frankenheimer and Lightner, became a real estate agent with Dr. Joseph Jarvis, and subdivided his property. From this and other real estate speculations he made some quick profits during the land boom which was sweeping all of southern California.

With his 1887 plan accepted he developed a domestic water system for the city, eliminating the open ditches, windmills, and water tanks in the downtown area. He formed the Rubidoux Hotel Association with A. S. White as president; L. M. Holt, secretary; O. T. Dyer, treasurer; and Jarvis, Dr. C. J. Gill, S. C. Evans, and himself as directors. Stock was sold to the public and $125,000 obtained or pledged.[12] Rosenthal let it be known he expected financial assistance from some wealthy friends and relatives (Baldwin?) but it did not materialize.

By August contractor A. W. Boggs, working from plans drawn by Architect John C. Pelton, Jr., began construction of a hotel on a site

12. *Ibid*, July 23, 1887

Mrs. Emil Rosenthal

above Pepper Street between Ninth and Eleventh. With the exception of the Hotel del Coronado, it was to be the biggest and most palatial hotel in southern California.

The elaborate design of the building with its 240 guest rooms was in a style described as a "combination of English, Gothic, and Swiss with a touch of Old Holland."[13] A picturesque driveway would lead up to the hotel which would overlook the city. The sum of $42,800 was spent on plans, foundations, roads, and framing before the boom's collapse halted all work. Under the leadership of L. M. Holt another attempt in 1891-92 to finish the hotel failed and Rosenthal lost all his property through foreclosure.

The Riverside Banking Company, which had loaned Rosenthal over $10,000 on unsecured notes and other funds to the Rubidoux Hotel Association, took over the construction site. The Pacific Mutual Life Insurance Company foreclosed on Rosenthal's Riverside Improvement Association which owned the Rubidoux Heights subdivision. On June 8, 1892 all hope for finishing the hotel vanished and the Press reported that "E. Rosenthal and family removed to Los Angeles yesterday where they will reside in the future." The family, now with six children, had lost everything.[14]

Others in Riverside also lost heavily but the Riverside Banking Company and O. T. Dyer suffered the most. The unfinished wood framing and the granite blocks of the hotel's foundation could be seen for years. Tom at his job may have foreseen disaster ahead for the bank.

Fortunately Riverside during this period had another bank which was financially sound. It was called the Riverside First National Bank and was located in the Castelman Block on the southeast corner of Main and Eighth streets, one block north of the Riverside Banking Company. On the corner windows of the main floor one could read "First National Bank, A. H. Naftzger, president; L. C. Waite, vice-president; A. Haeberlin, cashier; J. S. Castleman, assistant cashier. Founded in 1885." Soon, however, Riverside would have a third bank.

In April, 1890 Milton J. Daniels, a former Rochester, Minnesota bank president and state senator, arrived in Riverside. He came for his health and bought ten acres of citrus on Brockton Avenue north of Jurupa. There he built a fine, large home and began to talk about founding a bank.

The newspaper announced on July 3, 1891 that the Orange Growers Bank with M. J. Daniels as president had incorporated with $250,000

---

13. *Riverside Press and Horticulturist*, Oct. 1, 1887.
14. Esther Klotz, "Architects of Riverside's Building Boom 1886-93." *Report*. Riverside Museum Associates. Oct. 1967.

The Hayt Building, 1891

capital. Directors were George Frost, H. W. Huston, J. D. McNab, C. M. Loring, W. S. Sweat, J. R. Newberry, W. P. Lett, and G. Rouse with Frank Miller and W. Hayt listed among others as stockholders. A few weeks later the directors announced: "After careful deliberation and investigation H. T. Hays has been selected cashier and D. H. Herlihy, assistant cashier and bookkeeper. Hays' record is spotless and his ability of the highest order." Soon after his appointment as cashier Tom went to San Francisco on bank business. When he returned to Riverside a few weeks later he brought attractive orange-colored bank stationery and checks. They were engraved with pictures of orange trees in full fruit.[15]

In the meantime the bank's directors had arranged to lease the main floor of the Hayt Building located on the southwest corner of Main and Seventh streets. Since 1882 this brick business block owned by William Hayt had housed the Fashion Stables which were managed by his son Charles Hayt and S. K. Kleinfelter. In 1885 the structure had been greatly enlarged to accommodate more horses and livery equipment. Now, the building under the direction of Riverside architect, A. C. Willard, was being remodeled again. A third floor was added and the building extended to the alley. On the corner front of the second and third floors contractor H. A. Westbrook constructed a new round

15. *Riverside Daily Press*, Sept. 25, 1891.

tower to house the Knights of Pythias Lodge.[16]

On October 21, 1891 the Orange Growers Bank officially opened. President Daniels, George Frost, Herlihy, and Hays greeted and showed the visitors through the tastefully decorated rooms. Rich wallpapers and moldings made a background for the solid oak counters and furniture. On the ceiling at the corners of the paper panels were attached colorful plaster oranges and green leaves.[17] These were considered "strinkingly handsome and entirely in keeping with the bank's name." The big new safe was declared to be undoubtedly the best in town. With these fine quarters and such prominent officials success seemed assured.

---

16. *Riverside Daily Press*, Oct. 15, 1891.
17. *Ibid*, Oct. 17, 1891.

ORANGE GROWERS BANK

Subscribed Capital $250,000.

Riverside, Cal. Feb. 14 189

To whom it may concern:

This letter will serve to introduce Mr. H W Bordwell one of our most trust worthy citizens who represents the thoroughly reliable tree nursery firms of Riverside and vicinity. Mr. Bordwell is one of our most influential business men, and any courtesy shown him, will be much appreciated.

Very respectfully

[signature]

Tom writes a letter of recommendation.

CHAPTER III

Up The Social Ladder
or Pleasures and Pastimes

The Loring Building on the northwest corner of Main and Seventh streets was constructed in 1889. A spacious brick block, costing $75,000, it housed the Loring Opera House in the west wing, shops on the ground floor, and the City Hall, municipal courts, Riverside Free Library, and the Riverside Water Company in other rented space. The third floor had a few leased apartments. Into one of these soon after they came to Riverside Tom moved his wife Bertha and their new daughter Wanda.[1]

Charles M. Loring since 1885 had been a winter visitor from Minneapolis who always stayed at the Glenwood. He urged construction of the Loring Building and offered to help finance it so that Riverside could have an opera house. In 1889 a stock company with S. C. Evans as president was incorporated and work begun on the building, designed by A. C. Willard and J. M. Wood, the theatre architect from Chicago. Directors for the first two years were A. S. White, W. A. Hayt, F. A. Miller, T. E. Langley, I. W. Blum and C. M. Loring.[2]

When it was finished in January, 1890 Riverside had one of the most elegant opera houses in southern California. On the main floor and the two balconies turkey red velvet rugs carpeted the boxes, loges, aisles, and foyer. The 894 metal frame seats were well upholstered and

1. Information Mrs. J. S. Bordwell, 1966.
2. *Riverside Press and Horticulturist*, July 18, 1891.

The Loring Building

the light fixtures could use either gas or electricity. A large fireproof asbestos curtain and steel doors protected the stage which had a trap door cut in the floor through which "His Infernal Majesty" could emerge. A larger opening had a tank so that real boats could be seen sailing on real water.[3]

Frank Miller managed the Loring Opera Company and local talent produced on January 8th the first performance, *Iolanthe.* Under Miller's direction many outstanding programs followed. His acquaintance with Walter Raymond and other important hotel men enabled him to add the local house to a California opera circuit.

In December, 1891 Miller signed a contract to manage also the San Bernardino Opera House which was then being altered under the supervision of architect J. M. Wood who had worked on the Loring. When completed it too would be on this theatre circuit which included the Baldwin Theatre of San Francisco, the Los Angeles Grand Opera House, San Diego's new Fisher Opera, and Riverside's Loring.[4]

Some of Riverside's outstanding programs included *Faust,* played on January 1, 1891 by the Emma Juck Grand Opera Company. At this second grand opening opera seats sold as high as $7.50 and Hawaii's

3. *Riverside Daily Press,* Jan. 9, 1890.
4. *Riverside Press and Horticulturist,* Dec. 6, 1891.

From "Home of the Orange" 1893   *The Loring Opera House*

King Kalakua and suite were in attendance. The play was a great success.

On February 28th Frederick Wade, the great tragedian, played *Macbeth*. Miss Veronica Jarbeau and her new Gavotte Chorus of handsome girls performed on May 8th. They caused some consternation in certain local circles. The *Press* reported "Ladies in tights are objectionable! We think the exhibition of women in tights on stage can serve no good purpose and tends to the demoralization of young men and boys. The fact that the gallery was crowded to suffocation while the lower part of the house only half-full, when such a show is given, is proof that the better class of citizens desire something more refined."[5]

Frances Burnett's play *Little Lord Fauntleroy*, produced May 28th, must have met the city's standards as it was hailed as "one of the greatest

5. *Riverside Daily Press*, May 9, 1891.

Frank A. Miller, 1893

theatrical successes of modern times with no purer or better play ever put on stage." Many mothers attended with their young children who later appeared in velvet suits and lace collars like Fauntleroy. On September 11th, *Faust* was repeated, put on this time by the Lewis Morrison Company. It was called the best mounted play ever produced at the Loring. The stage sets were outstandingly beautiful.

James O'Neill's performance in *Monte Cristo* on the night of February 9, 1892 was never forgotten. This was followed two weeks later by *The Mikado*, a performance produced by Riversiders, with O. W. Kyle in the lead, Mable Castleman as Yum Yum, C. C. Trowbridge as Koko, and that popular and genial cashier of the Orange Growers Bank, Tom Hays, as Poo-Bah. The *Press* said he was magnificent in the part. "When he opened his mouth to sing there was a ripple of surprise which went around, for his voice is clear, deep, and powerful, true to tone,

Field Studios Collection   *Iolanthe, the first performance*

and musical to the ear. He sang and acted in the comic opera as though he had been for years on the boards. He has shown his hand (or rather his voice) and will be obliged to favor the public more."[6] The second performance, declared even better, drew a full house.

For one night only, November 26, 1892, Julia Marlowe played in Shakespeare's *Twelfth Night*. Her performance was brilliant but some people complained that Frank Miller should not have distributed his Keeley Institute folders along with the programs. This organization, strongly supported by Miller, worked hard against all forms of alcoholism and drugs.

On November 13, 1894 Tom played Dick Dead Eye, the deformed sailor, in *Pinafore* which starred Riverside's Marcia Craft as Buttercup.[7] Tom's role as Colonel Calverly in *Patience*, produced in February, 1895,

6. *Riverside Daily Press*, Feb. 27, 1892.
7. Marcia changed to Marcella after her European tour.

THE ARLINGTON HOTEL,

CENTRALLY LOCATED.   **RIVERSIDE, CAL.**

THIS hotel was erected in 1888 and is a model of elegance and neatness. It is richly furnished throughout and for home-like comfort and convenience has but few equals on the Pacific Coast. The house is comfortable in all of its appointments, the rooms are large and well ventilated and the table is always provided with the choicest of everything that can be found in the markets. Prompt and efficient service is characteristic of this hostelry. The building is lighted with incandescent lights, it is provided with a fine passenger elevator and all modern conveniences.

Terms Reasonable.   European and American Plan.

H. B. EVEREST,

PROPRIETOR.

☞ One of the finest BARBER SHOPS in Southern California is connected with the hotel.

pleased everyone, especially when he sang "When I first put this uniform on." However, C. C. Trowbridge as Reginald Bunthorne stole the show. The talented O. W. Kyle staged these productions with Mr. Ohlmeyr's orchestra of local musicians accompanying them, greatly adding to the show's entertainment.

Another activity of Tom's was the Riverside Lawn Tennis Club which was organized in the fall of 1892 with him as president; George Bittinger, vice-president; and Arthur Everest, secretary. They played on four tennis courts built by H. B. Everest, father of Arthur, on land just west of his big Arlington Hotel which stood on the northwest corner of Lime and Seventh streets.[8]

This hotel, considered Riverside's biggest and most beautiful building, was designed by Los Angeles architect Burgess C. Reeve and constructed in 1888 at a cost of $75,000.[9] An annex built in 1891 contained additional rooms and an electric generator for lighting. Benches, clothes hooks, and two shower baths were installed by the Tennis Club in these rooms. On the wall the club posted these rules. NO SUNDAY PLAYING, NO PLAYING WITH HIGH HEELED SHOES, ONLY ONE SET OR 13 GAMES IF MEMBERS WERE WAITING, AND THE LAST PLAYER MUST PICK UP THE BALLS. Sometimes the members, which included the Chase brothers who were excellent players, went out to Casa Blanca for a tournament and tea. Later H. B. Everest would entertain the team members and their wives at a fine Arlington Hotel dinner.

The Casa Blanca Tennis Club had been established in 1883 with

---

8. *Riverside Press and Horticulturist*, Sept. 24, 1892.
9. *Ibid*, Jan. 5, 1889.

Harry B. Lockwood, president, and James Bettner, vice-president.[10] Members played on the tennis courts at the rear of Lockwood's home on Magnolia and Adams streets. His house, called the Casa Blanca, was used to entertain the members until February, 1895 when a small club-house was built.[11]

Field Studios Collection   *Rubidoux Building at Seventh and Main*

In 1891 Tom joined the Rubidoux Club, the city's finest club for men, and on March 4, 1892 he became a director. Founded in 1888 with 40 members it moved a year later into its first regular quarters in the Cosmopolitan Block on the northeast corner of Eighth and Orange streets. There in four comfortable rooms members could play cards, billiards, or read the latest magazines such as *Puck, Judge,* and *Leslie's Illustrated Weekly.* Over the doorway hung a sign INTOXICATING LIQUORS OR GAMBLING OF ANY DESCRIPTION SHALL NOT BE ALLOWED IN THE CLUBROOMS. The club emphasized the social and cultural qualities of literary, historical and musical subjects, and two or three times a year held a ladies' night. Discussions on politics and religion were not allowed.[12]

10. *Ibid*, Dec. 15, 1883.
11. *Ibid*, Feb. 23, 1895.
12. *Riverside Press and Horticulturist,* May 25, 1889.

Photo by L. J. Klotz   *Tom's Sixth Street House*

In the spring of 1892 when the new Rubidoux building at the south-east corner of Main and Seventh was finished the Rubidoux Club was moved into seven rooms on the second floor. Membership, now over 100, included Riverside's most important business men. C. H. Keys was president. The board of directors included C. H. Loring, F. Miller, O. Backus, H. W. Bordwell, H. H. Monroe, M. J. Twogood, A. S. White, C. T. Rice, J. VandeGrift, J. S. Castleman, R. D. Osborn, A. C. Willard, and Tom who organized the musical programs, audited the books, and was in charge of billiards. Other officers were M. J. Daniels and F. E. Abbott, vice-presidents; G. E. Howard, secretary; and J. H. Fountain, treasurer; with G. Rouse and A. A. Wood as general assistants.[13]

Over 500 invitations were sent out for the club's formal opening of its new rooms on the evening of May 28, 1892. The party "elegant in every respect" was attended by over 400 people who danced to the Los Angeles Hungarian Orchestra in the flower-decorated rooms. Members viewed the club's growing collection of paintings and etchings. On the parlor wall a huge photograph of a London Zoo lion entitled *Majesty* gazed straight at you. Fine etchings of Venetian interiors and delicate

13. *Riverside Daily Press*, June 3, 1892.

maidens framed by sunsets and pastoral scenes were admired. One painting entitled A *Voice from the Cliff* by Winslow Homer and another called *Dash for Timber* by Frederic Remington were considered very fine. The only disappointment during the evening was that "due to unforeseen difficulties" the refreshments never arrived.[14]

In 1892 Tom moved his family from their Loring Building apartment into an attractive new, two-story house at 360 Sixth Street.[15] Here they gave small, intimate parties known for their sophistication. They were moving in the best circles.

14. *Riverside Reflex*, May 7, 1892.
15. *Riverside Directory*, 1893.

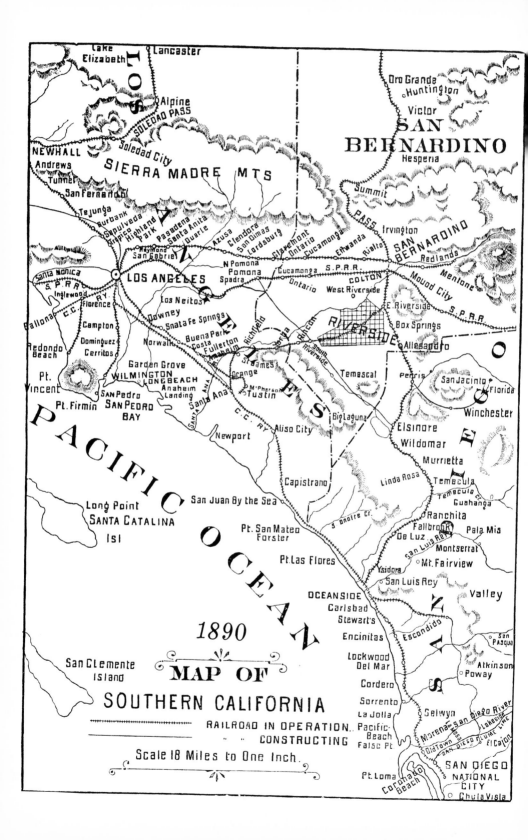

1890

MAP OF

SOUTHERN CALIFORNIA

RAILROAD IN OPERATION.
CONSTRUCTING

Scale 18 Miles to One Inch.

CHAPTER IV

Hard Times

In January, 1892 a severe frost destroyed half of the orange crop.[1] During 1891 the downright crookedness of the fruit commission men together with high freight rates brought only red ink for many of the citrus growers. Suddenly in July, 1892 all building seemed to stop with the completion of the Evans Bank Building and the Rubidoux Block. On November 19, 1892 lumber prices dropped sharply. J. E. Porter, the contractor on the Rubidoux Building, ran into financial troubles, could not pay his workmen, and finished the building with difficulty. These two business blocks were the last to be built for some years.

Prior to the decline in building, Riverside had erected eight fine business blocks and 150 homes. Due largely to profits from the new navel orange industry, the city remained relatively prosperous while other southern California cities suffered severely with the collapse of the 1887 boom. In 1890 the purchase of the Gage Canal and a thousand acres of its adjoining lands by an English syndicate, called the Riverside Trust Company Ltd.,[2] brought an influx of wealthy English settlers to develop the area southeast of Riverside. This greatly enhanced local prosperity.

1. *Riverside Daily Press*, Sept. 1, 1892.
2. *Ibid*, Mar. 14, 1890.

Evans Building under construction

Riverside Municipal Museum Collection

In July, 1891 about the time the Orange Growers Bank was organized, another bank called the Riverside National Bank was incorporated with $100,000 capital. Officers included S. C. Evans, Jr., president; S. C. Evans, vice-president; Francis H. Ross, cashier; and Pliny Evans, assistant cashier.

S. C. Evans, Jr.   M. J. Daniels

A new building was begun in December, 1891 on the northeast corner of Main and Eighth streets to house the Riverside National Bank, the Riverside Savings and Loan Association, and the Evans Commercial Company, all under the control of the S. C. Evans family. Since 1876 this family, operating as the Riverside Land and Water Company, had controlled extensive land and water interests in Riverside, principally south of Arlington Avenue. Their new building, designed by San Francisco architects Wright and Sanders, was constructed by local contractor H. A. Westbrook at a cost of $100,000. Its two-storied walls, formed with granite blocks from the Casa Blanca quarry and local brick, were 22 inches thick.

After seven months of construction the Evans Building opened on July 29, 1892. People attending the opening visited the Riverside National Bank with its solid mahogany counters, spacious vaults, safety deposit boxes, and directors' and cashier's offices, all of which occupied the

Bordwell Photo, Field Studios   *California Motor Road*

Eighth Street wing which had a corner entrance. To the east were the rooms of the Riverside Savings and Loan Company, the Evans' Company office, a stairway to the second floor, and three shop rooms to be rented.

Fronting on Main Street was a large shop room and a wide stairway which led to the 24 rooms on the second floor. These would be occupied by physicians, dentists, and lawyers. In the tower an electrically operated fire alarm bell was placed for the city's protection. It did not prove practical, however, as being too tightly enclosed in the tower it could not be heard.

The Riverside newspaper, called the *Phoenix,* described the building as "Massive and ornamental in exterior design; constructed most substantially and thoroughly in every detail of stone, iron and brick; with interior arrangements unexcelled for convenience, comfort and beauty; it commands the admiration and pride of all Riverside."[3] Few local buildings had been as well built.

In spite of these two new banks, business did not improve in 1893 and on June 16th big *Press* headlines announced the failure of the city's oldest bank, the Riverside Banking Company, where Tom had been employed. Manager O. T. Dyer stated that resources were $800,000 with capital stock at $429,000 held by 45 local shareholders.

---

3. The *Riverside Phoenix*, July 30, 1892.
   The Evans Bank was unfortunately demolished the summer of 1964.

A week later San Francisco's Pacific Bank having made extensive loans to Dyer and his bank, also failed. It had loaned the California Motor Road $40,600 and the Colton Marble and Lime Company $20,000 at a time when both companies were heavily in debt to the Riverside Banking Company.[4] In the meantime, banks throughout California and the United States were closing. The severe 1893 panic was underway and its effects would be felt for many years.

A committee of 15 Riverside businessmen undertook to straighten out the affairs of the Riverside Banking Company. A report made to stockholders and depositors gathered in the Loring Opera House stated that the estimated true value of the bank's resources was $498,672 rather than $800,000 and the immediate cause of the failure was believed to be due to rumors against O. T. Dyer's management.[5] In the fall of 1892, he was personally in debt to his own bank for real estate loans and in December he had mortgaged his personal real estate at other banks to repay his own bank and had lost in the transactions. The investigating committee reported that in spite of these difficulties it found rumors affecting Dyer's integrity wholly unfounded. With time they hoped a reorganization could be effected.[6]

During the same month the Orange Growers Bank pointed out its soundness, noting an increase in deposits. On July 1st Cashier Tom Hays announced a four percent dividend on paid up capital and also the hiring of James Goodhue, former cashier of the Riverside Banking Company. Tom had made a wise move when he left that bank two years earlier. No doubt at that time he saw its over extended condition.

In January, 1894, the Riverside Banking Company paid off almost $20,000 to depositors of $50 or less and O. T. Dyer deeded in trust to the bank his house and groves then valued at $110,000. Bank President A. Keith thanked the people for their patience during the hard times and announced a resumption of business under a limited depositors' contract.[7] However, with their money unobtainable most depositors experienced a difficult period.

That same month the city trustees were faced with the problem of local unemployment and an influx of poor and hungry people from a hard, cold, eastern winter. Tramps at first were arrested for vagrancy and kept in jail from three to ten days, but later a better system was tried. Men needing work would each be given three meal tickets and a night's lodging for a day's work helping to pave Riverside's muddy streets; they dug the

---

4. *Riverside Daily Press*, June 24, 1893.
5. *Ibid*, June 21, 1893.
6. *Ibid*, June 22, 1893.
7. *Riverside Daily Press*, Jan. 10, 1894.

gravel, worked in the Fairmount Quarry, and did roadwork. Priestly Hall, who lost some $16,000 worth of his 1887 real estate subdivision due to foreclosure by the Pacific Mutual Life Insurance Company, was put in charge of this Labor Bureau. One of the main jobs was to improve the Box Springs road east of town by reducing its grade from ten to five percent. John Hall, father of Priestly Hall, contracted the work using 64 men from the Labor Bureau. Half of their number were local residents who were paid one dollar a day while the transients received only the meal and lodging tickets.[8]

Frank Miller speaking in favor of the project said he would rather turn off the nine electric street lights, close the library, and eliminate street sprinkling than release these poor men from work. Since during

Priestly Hall

8. *Ibid*, Jan. 20 ,1894.

March the Labor Bureau's roll had increased to 118 men, he suggested that they pave Main Street.[9]

The severe eastern winter also sent to Riverside wealthy people escaping the ice and snow. A railroad passenger rate war in February, 1894 cut single fares from Chicago to Los Angeles to $32 and round trip fares to $55. The four local hotels: the Glenwood Tavern, the Arlington, the Rowell (a businessman's hotel on Main Street at Ninth), and the Anchorage were filled. The Glenwood was the most popular as Frank Miller knew well how to keep his guests comfortable and entertained. Mr. Rubenstein, the hypnotist, was then giving a series of demonstrations in the Glenwood parlors for the amusement of the visitors.

The Arlington Hotel had only 35 rooms available for tourists, the rest of this three-storied hotel serving as the Riverside County Courthouse. Owner H. B. Everest had leased some of the hotel for county offices in 1893 when Riverside County was formed out of portions of San Bernardino and San Diego Counties. He had had a stiff fight with Frank Miller who wanted the courthouse to occupy the new YMCA Building which stood on his block next to the Glenwood Tavern. Due to poor business conditions Everest offered very favorable terms and in July won the county lease.

Hard times no doubt caused the October 27, 1894 headline which told that the Evans Bank, named the Riverside National, would consolidate with the Orange Growers Bank. No explanations were given. The Orange Growers Bank announced it would move into the elegant quarters of the Evans Building and would handle all affairs of the Riverside National which would retire from business. S. C. Evans, Jr., former president of the absorbed National Bank, would become vice-president of the merged bank and M. J. Daniels would continue as president. H. T. Hays, cashier, would be assisted by J. H. Goodhue, formerly cashier of the Riverside National. This change would not affect the Riverside Savings and Loan Association which would continue unchanged with its headquarters in the Evans Building.

With this move Tom now had a fine private cashier's office opening onto the area behind the bank's main counters. The office was "a model of cozy comfort" with a glazed tile hearth and open coal grate, Brussels carpet, a mahogany desk, leather chairs, and both electric and gas lights.

The city received another shock three months later when the Riverside Water Company declared itself bankrupt. It had lost its capital reserve of $43,000 in the failure of the Riverside Banking Company and

9. *Riverside Daily Press*, Feb. 7, 1894.

W. H. Backus Photo
Courtesy Florence Backus

The Dyer House

now could not meet its interest payments. Due to the condition of the financial markets its bonds were difficult to sell. The court appointed George Frost as receiver to take charge of the bankruptcy. Customers of the Water Company were told that service would continue as usual.[10]

In the meantime, Otis T. Dyer continued to work on the problems of the Riverside Banking Company, foreclosing on some of its overdue property loans. In January, 1895 he met the 15 percent payout due depositors under their contract, thus distributing over $40,000 in cash. The previous year the bank had resumed business under a depositors' contract and issued certificates of deposit which bore interest and a promise of gradual payout. One troublesome event was a lawsuit by the First National Bank of Los Angeles against the bank for payment of a $35,600 loan. This loan constituted one-half of the Riverside Banking Company's liabilities other than those to stockholders.[11]

A year later in December, 1895 the State Board of Bank Commissioners turned over the remaining assets of the Riverside Banking Company to its Board of Directors for liquidation. By that time, however, the First National Bank of Los Angeles had foreclosed on much of the property and now owned the Riverside Banking Company's building, adjacent lots, and its property in the Tibbets Tract.[12] The Riverside Water Company acquired the Rubidoux Mountain hotel site which had been devel-

10. *Riverside Press and Horticulturist,* Jan. 12, 1895.
11. *Ibid,* Jan. 5, 1895.
12. *Riverside Press and Horticulturist,* Dec. 14, 1895.

oped by Emil Rosenthal during the boom and in June, 1904 would build a reservoir there.

During 1896 and 1897 the Riverside Banking Company continued a slow liquidation but in the spring of 1898 the directors announced assets of only $8,000 and liabilities of $300,000 still due depositors. It was evident there was no chance to pay out.[13]

Dyer had deeded to the bank his 20 acre orange grove and personal home on Main near Eleventh Street as a guarantee until some bank loans were collected. This property, valued at $110,000 in 1893 and now considered worth only $35,000, was returned to Dyer when the specific bank loans were collected. This resulted in a law suit against the bank by F. O. Lathrop, a depositor who had lost heavily. He wished to compel the Dyers to return the property to the liquidating bank. On July 30, 1898 Judge Noyes rendered a decision in the court case saying the bank was justified in returning the property to the Dyer family. Two weeks later, on August 15th, Otis T. Dyer, Riverside's first banker who had employed Tom on his arrival in Riverside, died of diabetes, aged 54. He left a wife Mary, two married daughters, a sister Miss E. C., and a brother, L. L. Dyer. The newspaper praised O. T. Dyer's ability, generosity, and progressiveness but made no mention of the still unsettled affairs of his bank.

The final chapter in the history of this pioneer bank occurred February 11, 1899 when Sheriff Johnson sold the remaining assets at auction. A *Press* headline read "Much for little. Assets of Riverside Banking Company go for a song". These assets were mostly notes, mortgages, and capital stock of defunct companies. W. S. Collins bought for a total of $2.50 two-thirds of the outstanding stock of the Palm Valley Land Company which had owned 300 acres of desert land near present day Palm Springs. A lot of 163 shares of the Colton Marble and Lime Company brought five cents and P. S. Dinsmore acquired 4,000 shares of the San Bernardino Artificial Stone Company for a dime. An unsecured Emil Rosenthal note for $10,461 also went for a nickel while a $17,000 note from the California Motor Road sold for 55 cents. Other notes and mortgages sold for similarly ridiculous prices.

---

13. *Ibid,* June 25, 1898.

BANANA PLANT.

CHAPTER V
Orange Day

Tom's political activities which later were to prove so important, began in the spring of 1894. In March he was included in a list of delegates attending the state Republican convention. In June he was elected president of a new active Young Men's Republican Club which had 150 members and twice monthly met at the Armory Hall. M. J. Daniels often spoke to the group, his jovial humor and large repertory of witty jokes making him popular with the young men.[1]

Tom introduced music using political parodies to such tunes as "Tit Willow" or "Ta-ra-ra-ra Boom-de-ay". This greatly added to the success of the meetings and Tom proved to be an able and well-liked president. His enthusiasm brought in new members and before long similar clubs formed in San Jacinto, Elsinore, and other towns in the county. With several Riverside members Tom would take the train to go to speak at these county rallies. S. C. Evans, Jr. and John G. North, seeking important political offices, also spoke at these political meetings. Because of the hard times and unemployment many speakers promised improved business conditions and "the full dinner pail". This last slogan would assume great importance in the William McKinley presidential campaigns of 1896 and 1900.

---

1. *Riverside Press and Horticulturist*, June 30, 1894.

White Park and Bandstand

In the spring of 1895 business conditions in Riverside began to improve slowly. Fewer transients needed work and Priestly Hall returned to his nursery business. There had been no frost injury to citrus the past winter and the crop was abundant and of excellent quality. Thanks largely to the work of the new Southern California Fruit Exchange, prices had also improved.

The city looked better with a few more paved streets and sidewalks and the city's park, formerly a swamp, was now a beauty spot. After two years of hard work by Riverside's Board of Park Commissionners headed by A. S. White, Bradford Morse, and J. A. Simms, the place had been transformed. The little bandstand which stood near the center was now surrounded by new gravel walks, flowers, shrubs, and cacti installed by head gardner Adolph Scheffler under the direction of the well known landscape architect Franz Hosp.[2] Some of the cacti were very unusual, especially the great cactus (*Cereus gigantius*) which eastern visitors found so interesting.

The Riverside Water Company's lower canal flowed through the park in a cemented ditch and many attractive little bridges crossed this canal adding interest to the gardens. The fountain, which had long stood half-finished, was completed. Nearby was the rose garden with 200

2. Mary Scott, "Franz P. Hosp." Report: Riverside Museum Associates, May, 1966.

Magnolia Ave., Riverside, Cal.

varieties collected and planted by Hosp and White. This park, designated in October, 1899 by the city trustees as Albert S. White Park, was named for this man who made almost daily visits to view its growth. Developed on two city blocks on the west side of Market Street and south of Eighth Street, it became famous for its cactus garden.[3]

Local people anxious to keep the city attractive complained to the city trustees that there was too much tobacco juice spitting by the unemployed men who hung around the street corners, especially at Eighth and Main. They pointed out that Pomona had an anti-spitting ordinance. At that time there seemed to be no reply from the city fathers but on January 11, 1901, six years later, they adopted a "No Spitting Ordinance." Frank Miller, who managed the local street car system, urged its passage and said he would see that a thousand copies of the ordinance were distributed. No doubt there were problems in keeping the street cars clean as tobacco chewing was a common practice. Other complainers led by Nurseryman D. C. Twogood protested the cutting down of all the old pepper trees that lined Eighth Street from Main Street east to the railroad tracks. Twogood said the beauty of these old trees that had taken years to grow could not be replaced.

Magnolia Avenue running south some seven miles was a beautiful unpaved double roadway lined with quality homes and magnolia, cypress,

3. *Riverside Press and Horticulturist*, Nov. 24, 1894.

Bordwell Photo   *Orange Day, Main and Eighth*

pepper, palm, and eucalyptus trees growing above clipped box hedges. A small mule-drawn trolley car carried passengers along the center strip of the street. The avenue, always well photographed, was usually featured in articles on the area.

Most of the townspeople welcomed a new 1894 city ordinance which confined the Chinese laundry work to Chinatown.[4] No longer would the local Chinese, who did most of the household and agricultural labor, be allowed to hang the laundry over the downtown rooftops to flap in the breeze over the city's streets. No longer were they permitted to wash in the deep flowing gutters of the business district.

The Chinese, forced out of the downtown area in 1886, relocated on Brockton Avenue in the Tequesquite Arroyo. On July 31, 1893 a serious fire destroyed most of their cheap wooden shacks. Chinatown was rebuilt with more attractive and safer brick buildings.[5] These housed about 400 Chinamen including one small family, for on September 26, 1891 Mr. and Mrs. Chung Gee rejoiced over the first Chinese baby to be born in Riverside. This little boy was quite a curiosity.

In April, 1895 Riverside celebrated her good orange crop with the city's first "Orange Day" held on Monday, the 22nd. Almost everyone served on a committee. Frank Miller had proposed the idea and arranged

4. *Ibid*, Dec. 1, 1894.
5. Harry Lawton, *Riverside Pioneer Chinese* (Press-Enterprise, 1959).

This elegant Victorian mansion built in 1891 by Mrs. James Bettner, widowed mother of Robert L. Bettner, is located at 8193 Magnolia Avenue. It is one of the few surviving examples of the affluent homes which lined the Avenue. Tall chimneys, glazed tile fireplaces, beautiful wood turnings and narrow shuttered windows reflect the period.

The house was designed by the distinguished architect John A. Walls of the Los Angeles firm of Morgan and Walls and cost $11,000. In May, 1893 contractor John Hanlon filed a lawsuit against Mrs. Bettner for $440. A disagreement arose over payment for extra work which included a back stairway, a higher brick foundation and a corral. The contractor was awarded $295 which was considered reasonable. Thanks to this court case, discovered by the author, the early history of the house is known.

In 1969 under the leadership of Mrs. Stewart D. Button the Riverside Museum Associates purchased the house. It is being restored under the direction of designer F. Carl Fowler and on completion will be presented to the city as Riverside's Heritage House.

for special railroad trains and fares for the day. He issued a special invitation to San Francisco's new Half Million Club and 80 members arrived on two special trains of nine cars each which also brought other San Franciscans. The main purpose of this club was to promote the growth of San Francisco from a city of 300,000 to one of a half-million people. M. J. Daniels and Tom Hays made all arrangements for their lodging and entertainment.

Architects A. C. Willard and A. W. Boggs had designed and built a large arch over Main Street which spelled out "Welcome" in oranges. Merchants used oranges to decorate their windows and strung oranges on wires which went from tree to tree. Oranges were placed on lawns in intricate welcome sign patterns and private fountains were heaped with them. On the streets were placed orange boxes filled with the fruit to be eaten by visitors. Orange-colored ribbon streamers hanging from the buildings added a festive air. The Glenwood served excellent food all day featuring oranges and baskets filled with them hung in the main lobby and dining room. On the lawn "Welcome to the Glenwood Tavern" was written with the fruit.[6]

Band music greeted visitors arriving by train. A pretty girl thrust a navel orange into the arrival's hand and while he wondered what to do with it, another pretty girl put a boutonniere of orange blossoms in his lapel. The ladies received small orange blossom corsages which had been made by the school children. All during the day M. J. Daniels and Tom kept busy arranging for tallyho rides to the principal places and pointing out the beauty of Riverside to members of the Half Million Club. These and other visitors were welcomed at the public library, Loring Opera House, Armory Hall, Y.M.C.A., Knights of Pythias Castle, Masonic Temple in the Castleman Block, and the Odd Fellows Hall, all of which were kept open for the visitors' convenience.

The day's program consisted of short buggy trips down Magnolia Avenue to see beautiful homes such as those of S. C. Evans, Mrs. James Bettner, Mrs. L. S. Gilliland (Casa Grande), and O. T. Johnson. Another ride was to Priestly Hall's large adobe house called Rockledge which stood near the Victoria Bridge next to his nursery where young citrus trees, roses, and unusual flowering plants were for sale. Others drove to the Casa Blanca Lawn Tennis Club on Adams Street to see the matches and to have tea in the clubhouse. Some groups enjoyed a trip across Victoria Bridge and down the newly planted Victoria Avenue whose trees were then only three years old. Here they saw the Riverside Trust

---

6. *Riverside Press and Horticulturist*, April 27, 1895.

Casa Grande built in 1878 by James H. Benedict; it later became the home of the Gilliland family. Unfortunately the house was destroyed in 1955 after it had been beautifully restored by Robert Westbrook. It stood where Ramona high school now stands.

Riverside Municipal Museum Collection

Company's vast groves of young bearing orange trees and the Gage Canal system. Later a big parade featured the band, floats, and 212 stunting wheelmen decorated with flying orange streamers and dressed in sports attire. The bicyclists had come from all over southern California.

Many visitors remained overnight to attend the program at the Loring Opera that evening. David Belasco's play, *The Girl I Left Behind Me* had been advertised as "The Best American Play." It showed brave American soldiers and their girls at frontier forts contending with perilous Indian uprisings. Indian music and tom-tom drums added excitement to the well-staged professional performance.[7]

It was estimated that over 2,000 visitors, some of whom came long distances, attended the Orange Day celebration. Riverside received much publicity in the California newspapers, many of which had sent their reporters to cover the story.

---

7. *Ibid*, April 22, 1895.

A long lasting benefit to Riverside which resulted indirectly from Orange Day was the organization of the Riverside Horticultural Club. It held its first meeting on May 18, 1895 with Professor S. A. Cook of Pomona College as speaker. A month earlier John H. Reed, G. W. Garcelon, William Irving, E. L. Koethen, and James Boyd who had worked together on Orange Day arrangements met to discuss the formation of the club. The first officers were E. L. Koethen, president; W. Irving, vice-president; and J. P. Baumgartner, secretary and treasurer. The group arranged to meet monthly at the homes of various members to hear speakers informed on horticultural subjects and to discuss their common citrus problems.[8] This club would test methods for heating citrus orchards, irrigation, pest control, and packinghouse practices, all of which would greatly benefit southern California citrus growers.

8. *Ibid*, May 18, 1895.

CHAPTER VI

The City Out Of Mud and Darkness
Struggles with the Liquor Problem

In March, 1896 Tom Hays was elected president of the Rubidoux Club and was reelected in 1897 and 1898.[1] Since the club had moved into its new rooms in the Rubidoux Building in 1892 the organization had grown in prestige and popularity. Under Tom's leadership the club remained free from debt and began various new programs such as a well attended monthly smoker. This always featured music with Tom often singing solo parts or in a quartet which included Messrs. McBean, Shaw, and Stanton. Billiard tournaments played in the club rooms were greatly enjoyed with H. B. Chase, Geo. Bittinger, and Hays making top scores.

Tom organized the Rubidoux Club's Charity Minstrels and acted as interlocutor in their many performances before political and social clubs. Nine men in black face and dressed in green jackets, dark trousers, and white gloves provided popular and often hilarious entertainment. Their small earnings were used for the club's charity work.

As a member of the local Masonic Lodge Tom participated in a famous Cakewalk Party put on by the Ladies of the Order of the Eastern Star in February, 1896. Dressed as Juliet with pantalettes showing below

---

1. *Riverside Press and Horticulturist*, Mar. 14, 1896.

Fairchild Street Paving

a full skirt he and his partner, Ed Stanton, who was Romeo, won the cake in the grand finale which included 20 ridiculously dressed couples. Tom's pantalettes influenced the judges who proved susceptible to that "lady's" charm. Funds received from the party bought a new piano for the Masons.[2]

At Fourth of July celebrations, Memorial Day exercises, and political rallies, Hays was always in charge of music. This activity together with his growing political work increased his local importance. His position as president of the Young Republican Club also made him well known throughout the county. In July, 1896 this club changed its title to the McKinley and Hobart Club, named for the two Republican candidates in the coming November presidential election. Pember Castleman, son of the local banker J. S. Castleman, was elected president and Hays, treasurer.[3] In September, 1895 Pember returned from three years of law training in New York City and began practice in the Riverside courts. Having a good voice he worked with Tom not only at political meetings but also at the Rubidoux Club. In October, 1896 in a beautifully decorated All Saints Episcopal Church he married M. J. Daniels' daughter Maud.

Daniels during this period was still president of the Orange Growers Bank with S. C. Evans, Jr., vice-president; Tom Hays, cashier; and M. J. Twogood, assistant cashier. The bank had increased deposits and grown

---

2. *Ibid*, Feb. 1, 1896.
3. *Ibid*, July 4, 1896.

Ed E. Miller, in fireman uniform

in importance since it had moved into the Evans Building. Bank customers were usually greeted with a broad smile from Tom at the cashier's window. With a pencil over his right ear he looked very businesslike.

On January 25, 1896 S. C. Evans announced the liquidation of the Riverside Savings and Loan Association which occupied quarters to the rear of the Orange Growers Bank. The association paid off all depositors, retired from business, and released its rooms to the Orange Growers Bank. This gave it the finest quarters of any bank in southern California and the only bank in Riverside with safety deposit boxes.

Although Hays was very active in banking, music, and political work, he does not appear among the local men who were responsible in 1895 and 1896 for great city improvements. On June 6, 1895 the people voted overwhelmingly for bonds to keep Riverside "out of mud and darkness." The sum of $130,000 would pave many city streets and $40,000 would provide a new electric light system.

The work began in September, 1895 with the paving of Main Street from Sixth to Tenth with asphaltum which was preferred to macadam. By January, 1896 contractor J. A. Fairchild and his street crew had paved

13 blocks. The last to be finished on that contract was Eighth Street from Main to the Santa Fe tracks. The cost was $37,500 of which $26,000 was paid by the city and the rest by the property owners.[4] Due to the paving an unforseen difficulty developed with horses. The waterman continued to sprinkle the streets, paved or unpaved, and after the sprinkling many smooth-shod horses slipped and fell and sometimes it was difficult to get them back on their feet. A suggestion was made that it might be better to sweep than to water the paved streets.

Bordwell Photo

S. Masters Carriage Shop, Seventh and Market

Unfortunately, the paving did not prove very durable. By April, 1897 large ruts and holes had been caused by the heavy wagon wheels. Fairchild made some repairs but said the major difficulty was due to the city trustees' having specified a dirt foundation instead of rock. The city altered its road building plans and spent over $2,000 more for repairs. Cement sidewalks and granite curbs installed during the paving necessitated removal of many old trees. A long line of beautiful tall eucalyptus trees on the east side of Main Street south of Twelfth became firewood and all the cypress trees on the other side of Main Street in the Dyer Block and on Fourteenth had to be cut down.

When the street work began the city trustees saw the necessity of securing a source of rock for future pavings. Frank Miller appeared before the trustees with a list of donors willing to assist the city in buying the Fairmount Heights Hill Quarry to supply street rock. John G. North would sell it for $10,000. George Reynolds and M. J. Daniels said they

4. *Ibid*, Dec. 21, 1895.

thought the city should pay the required amount as it then would own five acres of rock quarry, ten acres of hill land, and 20 acres of alfalfa land with water rights which could be used for a park. The city would also acquire a right-of-way in Block 18 so that West Seventh Street could be opened to West Riverside.[5] Previously travelers went around south of Mt. Rubidoux to cross the river by bridge or ford. In September, 1895 the trustees voted to buy the property outright without citizens' help and asked for bids on a rock crusher which was expected to cost $2,500.

A little later S. C. Evans announced he would give five inches of water and 12 acres of adjoining land to enlarge the area to be used as a park. When over a hundred people honored him at a Glenwood Hotel banquet on November 9, 1895, M. J. Daniels spoke of Evans as the "Father of Riverside" and told of the city's plan to develop a lake on this promised site. However, not until 1903 did the city secure title to the property on a perpetual lease basis.

While the street paving was underway, Frank Miller had all his walks and driveways in his hotel block paved with asphalt. Earlier that year he had installed tennis and croquet courts, pool and billiard rooms, and enclosed and roofed a south veranda with glass so that his eastern guests could sunbathe in winter. In December Frank's brother, Ed Miller, bought for his Glenwood Stables a beautiful $600 four-seated tallyho which could carry 14 people. It had been built by S. Masters in his local carriage shop. Under the footrests were places for picnic baskets which often accompanied hotel guests on the all-day outings planned by Frank Miller.[6] These stables built on the southwest corner of Main and Sixth streets supplied the transportation needs of the Glenwood.

Although the bonds for the street paving and electric light plant had been voted in June, 1895 it took over a year to build the new electric stations and light the city. Earlier, Riverside had secured a limited amount of electricity from the San Bernardino Electric Light and Power Company which was organized in January, 1887 with J. G. Burt, president, and O. T. Dyer, vice-president.[7] Utilizing a fall in the upper canal of the Riverside Water Company for power, a small plant was built a mile south of East Riverside (now Highgrove). It produced its first current in February, 1887. After a decision by the City of Riverside to buy some of the power from this source, the company in March, 1888 began putting up poles in Riverside.[8] By April, 30 lights were in operation but few

5. *Ibid*, Sept. 21, 1895.
6. *Ibid*, Dec. 14, 1895.
7. *Riverside Daily Press*, Jan. 27, 1887.
8. *Riverside Press and Horticulturist*, Mar. 24, 1888.

were on the streets. This electricity was expensive and soon proved inadequate to meet the needs of the city.

On February 29, 1896 the city trustees announced it had accepted the bid of the California Electric Works of San Francisco for the construction of an electric system for Riverside. The Redlands Electric Light Company, whose powerhouse had 15 Pelton wheels in Mill Creek Canyon, would send electricity over new lines to Riverside. A brick electric building had been completed on Mulberry Street by contractor J. C. Masters. Three big 10,000 watt transformers were ready to receive the power in July.[9] Poles were set and wires strung, often leaving behind butchered street trees which brought complaints from the new Street Ornamentation Committee and irate residents.

When the lights went on in Riverside October 15, 1896, *Press* headlines read "Now we are Illuminated". In the downtown area 74 incandescent street lights shone and the first mile of Magnolia Avenue twinkled, lit by 50 light poles each with three 16 candlepower lights. The rest of the Avenue would have lights as soon as possible. For several weeks linemen hung wires to bring the new light to stores, homes, and the Glenwood Hotel which installed 130 lights, greatly pleasing its guests.

The *Riverside Daily Press* bought new electric machinery to operate its printing press and Frank Miller, manager of the Riverside and Arlington Street Railway, began to study how to electrify the city's street car line.[10] In the first few years there were frequent power breakdowns and people complained of their on-again, off-again lights. Before long, however, the city had a well-operated and comparatively cheap system. It paid less for its electricity than almost any other southern California city.

In recognition of their good work, a year later on October 30, 1897 the employees of the electric light company received a $10 monthly increase in pay. Manager Fred Worthley's salary was raised to $90, A. A. Davis to $75, George Brown to $75, F. C. Sweetser to $65, and those of Elmer Cutting, George Johnson, and W. Thompson each to $60 a month. These men were the pioneer employees of the city's electric system.

During this period of civic improvement the community had increasing difficulty in controlling the sale of alcoholic beverages. For some years after Riverside was incorporated in 1883 the city had a few saloons which paid a high yearly tax but in April, 1888 these were closed. In hotels with 40 or more rooms the sale of wine and beer was permitted with meals costing at least 25 cents.[11] This ordinance was proposed on

9. *Ibid*, Oct. 31, 1896.
10. *Ibid*, Oct. 10, 1896.
11. *Ibid*, July 31, 1897.

Holyrood Hotel, Market and Eighth

November 6, 1889 by Frank Miller, who although himself a prohibitionist knew the necessity of being able to furnish alcoholic refreshments to his hotel guests. When this ordinance went into effect only Miller's Glenwood Tavern could qualify, but by 1897 the Holyrood, Arlington, and the Magnolia Hotels also claimed more than 40 rooms. The inspecting city sheriff complained, however, that some rooms of the Magnolia Hotel which had been cut into two rooms in order to qualify for the liquor license, were so small they contained nothing but a cot.[12]

The Magnolia, a popular hotel for businessmen, was on the second floor of the new Burt Block located on the northwest corner of Main and Eighth streets. In July, 1897 Riverside lost one of its oldest landmarks when the 1875 Burt Building was torn down and a new structure with bay windows, tower, and cupola was built at the same location.[13]

With no saloons permitted, and with hotels regulated, more local liquor trade developed with the drugstores which were also allowed to sell alcohol. Tom, like anyone else who wished a beer with his lunch, could walk into the Sebrell, the Heath and Morrison, or Hardman Drugstores, go to the basement and have his beer. Or if he wished to drink it elsewhere, he could ask the main floor clerk for "one shoe or two shoes". The clerk would disappear for a moment and then return with a shoe

12. *Ibid*, Sept. 25, 1897.
13. *Ibid*, July 3, 1897.

box containing one or two bottles of beer.

Floyd H. Followell, then a boy fifteen years old, remembers Tom as a jovial, well-liked young man always in a hurry. Tom would enter the drugstore and call out to someone he knew to join him for a drink. Floyd said that he never accepted Tom's invitation for a beer even though it cost only ten cents a quart. Besides no liquor was sold to minors.[14]

This drugstore trade did not please the W.C.T.U. ladies and the local ministers who declared that the drugstore saloon system was a disgrace. Leading this fight was the Reverend Edward F. Goff, who since his arrival in June, 1896 had been an able and popular pastor of the First Congregational Church. Of Puritan stock and a descendant of Sir William Goffe who was one of Cromwell's generals, the Reverend Goff was a moral leader for the community as well as for his 350 church members.[15]

Nevertheless, the city trustees seemed to prefer the drugstore system to the open saloon. Almost nightly heavy wagons drawn by four horses arrived bringing beer, wine, and hard liquor from San Bernardino and Colton. They unloaded in the alleys, carrying in the bottled drinks and rolling the barrels of beer into the basement of the drugstores. Floyd Followell and other young boys would be called in from the street to help with the unloading and would receive fifty cents each for their work.

Also there seemed to be no prohibition of the manufacturing of wine in Riverside, for in February, 1896 an orange winery opened on Third Street near the railroad tracks. In a large two-storied building the wine was made from edible culls supplied by the local growers who were relieved of disposing of them. Machinery mashed the fruit from which juice was recovered. This was strained, sugar added, and the product placed in 12 large 2100 gallon tanks for fermentation. Amos Schultz, the local manager, employed 32 people who did the fruit sorting, juice mixing, and filling the wine kegs. After three to five weeks of fermenting the wine was shipped to the company's plants in Philadelphia where it was bottled and aged for two years.[16] One item concerning the winery was not mentioned in the *Press* story. In the vicinity one could smell the strong odor of rotting orange rinds and pulp which the company dumped on adjacent lots.

There is no record of any local tasting or drinking of this wine but one likes to think that the Riverside newspaper boys might have received a demijohn as a reward for a well-written story on the Riverside orange winery.

---

14. Interview with Floyd H. Followell of Riverside, 1971.
15. *Riverside Directory*, 1897.
16. *Riverside Press and Horticulturist*, Feb. 1, 1896.

CHAPTER VII

Bicycling, Polo and Golf

During his early Riverside years Tom was enthusiastic over tennis but in the nineties when bicycling became popular he joined his friends in promoting that sport. Although he may have ridden a bicycle there is no record that he joined in the long trips or the racing.

In the fall of 1891 Harry Hawes, a partner with his father N. S. Hawes, in a shop which sold pianos, sewing machines, picture frames, and bicycles, organized the Riverside Wheelmen. Officers were Harry Hawes, president; Arthur Everest, vice-president; and W. K. Cowan, secretary-treasurer. The club, which first consisted of ten "riders of the silent steed", met at the YMCA.[1] They often took a spin to such popular places as Glen Ivy in Temescal Canyon which had just installed "a large indoor swimming bath", or to Harlem Springs near Colton, or that popular resort, Eden Hot Springs near San Jacinto.

The bicycle and baseball boys, needing a place to practice their sports, gathered $700 in contributions, leased land on Third Street east of the railroad from L. V. W. Brown, and built a half-mile track. Called Athletic Park it was finished and dedicated in February, 1892. Then it was complete with a solid six-foot board fence and a small grandstand

---

1. *Riverside Press and Horticulturist*, Oct. 10, 1891.

Riverside Municipal Museum Collection   *Carl Derby (Arrow) in Bicycle Race*
Athletic Park, 1892

and was used not only for bicycling and baseball but other sports as well. Tom often watched the sports and acted as timer for the bicycle races.[2] Always involved in the center of activity, he seemed to prefer a job of authority.

Bicycling grew in popularity until many roads were made dusty by the wheels. Some women complained of the riders' scanty garments which they said looked like bathing suits. Men on the other hand, noting the new bifurcated skirts of the Ladies Spinning Club, a local wheel-womens' group, commented that before long women would be riding horses as well as bicycles man-style.

During the last three days of May, 1894 the Second Annual Meeting of the Southern California Division of Wheelmen held races at the San Diego Sweetwater Track. The eight Riverside wheelmen who took the long ride to participate, also enjoyed the parades, bicycle excursion to La Jolla Park, the races on the fast track, and the Grand Ball held at Hotel del Coronado. Riverside wheelman Harry E. Scott won one event and Casey Castleman won first prize in the mile, a $188 full nickel-plated Cleveland Racer bicycle. Tom and S. J. Castleman, who had spent much time helping to train the Riverside team, were elated over these successes.

Another never-to-be-forgotten trip of the Riverside Wheelmen was

---

2. *Riverside Daily Press*, Jan. 5, Jan. 21, 1892.

to the big Indian Fiesta at Temecula in August, 1894 which was attended by 1500 people. The events which lasted four days included bicycle, boat, and horse races, Indian games, war dances, and a baseball game between the Indians and the palefaces. Trujillo's Riverside horses won many of the races but the ball players quit in the third inning due to the heat. The bicycle riders looked hot, dusty, and wilted after their return trip to Riverside.

William J. Powell Photo   *A Lady Spinner*

On January 21, 1895 the Riverside Wheelmen incorporated with capital stock of $10,000 and announced that they had secured a seven acre tract near Fairmount Hill bounded by Pine, Houghton, Locust, and Second streets. The new place like the old abandoned one, was called Athletic Park. The committee in charge of the new park included W. A. Correll, J. A. Simms, I. S. Logan, S. J. Castleman, George Cobb, and Tom Hays who was treasurer.[3] Under their direction civil engineer Kingsbury Sanborn laid out a carefully graded third-mile oval track which was considered the finest in the area. A new 30-by-50-foot grandstand, usually decorated in the orange and black colors of the local team, afforded good viewing of all events.[4] Tom and the rest of the committee

---

3. *Riverside Press and Horticulturist*, May 14, 1895 and Aug. 7, 1897.
4. *Ibid*, July 20 and 27, 1895.

worked many hours to improve the facilities.

On September 9th the new park was opened with a big celebration. Wheelmen's clubs came from all the surrounding cities for a morning meeting at the Odd Fellows Hall and afternoon races at the new track. The Syracuse Cycling Club impressed the town with its red wheeled bicycles; wheels of other teams were also colorfully decorated. Events of the day included tandem, triplet, mile, and novice races, ending with a thrilling 25-mile event. This new track did much to increase the interest in wheel riding and racing.

I. S. Logan

During the next five years on Admission Day, September 9th, wheelmen invaded Riverside for important meets. On three of these years, 1896, 1897, and 1898, the local wheelmen under the leadership of Carson Shoemaker, Harry E. Scott and George B. Cox won the 25-mile team race. In October, 1898 Shoemaker, known as "Jasper" or "Shoe", won the mile race in 1:59. This record remained unbroken even after bike racing declined in popularity and Athletic Park was abandoned at the turn of the century.

Bordwell Photo   *Athletic Park Baseball Team*
Joe Bordwell fifth and Charles
Rouse sixth from the left, 1895

Other outstanding local stars of the wheel track were Casey Castle-man, Charlie and Jimmie Cowan, Albert Newcomb, Will Ruby, and Will Wasson. Cyclist George Cox, usually known as "Barty", was considered the pretty boy and a great favorite with the ladies. When Scott beat Castleman in 1894 he became a popular hero but none excelled Shoemaker. He won many races but his most unusual victory was when he took second in the 1896 Elsinore 17-mile road race finishing the last six miles on a flat tire.

Although used primarily by the wheelmen Athletic Park also became a popular place for baseball games and Fourth of July celebrations which often included fireworks and sack, egg, wheelbarrow, and three-legged races. Most local parades ended there for an afternoon of sports featuring lacrosse, turkey shoots, or ball games.

By 1897 Tom's name no longer appeared among those of Ike S. Logan, W. A. Correll, and others who did so much to promote the wheelmen. Instead he was spending more and more time on politics and golf. Sometime during 1897 Tom learned to play this game. By October, 1898 when the Rubidoux Club formed a golf auxiliary he was already a good player and thus it is reasonable to assume he played on Riverside's first important golf course built by the Riverside Polo Club.

Although it was an elite club Tom was never listed as a member.

The Riverside Polo Club, established in November, 1892 held its meetings in Arlington at the camp house of the Riverside Trust Company, Ltd. A year later the club had 14 members including R. Bettner, chairman; G. L. Waring, secretary; and W. P. Lett, R. Allen, G. Allen, H. L. Hughes, B. Gaylord, C. Baker, H. Maud, C. Maud, F. W. Fox, H. P. Woods, A. Hotson and Simpleton. The polo grounds occupied land leased from the Riverside Trust Company at Jefferson Street near the Casa Blanca railway station.[5]

In February, 1896 William Irving, president of the trust company, announced the necessity to run a new railway spur through the polo grounds along the side of the grandstand. Since this was not agreeable to the club members a month later they leased from the trust company a much larger site at the northwest corner of Victoria and Van Buren avenues. Here they built a five-eighths mile racetrack, a polo field, two croquet grounds, a tennis court, and a $500 clubhouse. In September, 1897 C. E. Maud supervised the construction of a first-class nine-hole golf course. The name was then changed to the Riverside Polo and Golf Club.[6]

The club celebrated the opening of its new grounds on December 26, 1896 with a racing meet, a polo game, and a tea served by wives of the members. In the first race Robert Bettner's pacer, Polo Maid, won by a neck over Duyckinck's trotter, Ben Smith. As the course was uphill the horses set no record. Bettner's Lady Peach won over C. E. Maud's Nancy Lee in another heat. The last race with seven ponies entered was most exciting with Bettner riding Kiss-Me-Quick to win. J. B. Norton on his pony, Thompson, was second, and M. E. Flowers on Wonder, third. The polo game started rather late and due to a bad wind the finish was inconclusive. Everyone, however, enjoyed the tea and praised the new grounds.[7]

In January, 1897 the club's officers President Dudley Duyckinck, vice-president C. E. Maud, secretary-treasurer P. E. White and captain of the polo team R. Bettner voted to include ladies as members. But something must have gone wrong because the motion was rescinded in March. A new rule stated that "only ladies of the immediate family of members may be admitted to honorary membership on being duly proposed, seconded, and elected by the committee." It is assumed if elected they would also pay the monthly memberships of $2.50 or $10 yearly dues.[8]

The Burlingame Polo Club in February, 1897 sent its 16 ponies by

5. *Riverside Polo Club Minutes.*
6. *Ibid.*
7. *Riverside Press and Horticulturist*, Dec. 26, 1896.
8. *Polo Club Minutes.*

Southern Pacific railway car for a match with the local team. Hall's Race Track in the Tequesquite Arroyo west of Chinatown, was equipped with a grandstand and horse stables. Laid out and built by John Hall in 1892 it had been used extensively by the city's horsemen. The Burlingame ponies were kept there until the afternoon of the polo game.[9] A double ring of carriages filled with Riverside's socially elite watched the match. The Riverside team of Bettner, Maud, Allen, and Norton dressed in black and red and appearing on their fine ponies were received with a yell of enthusiasm by the crowd. The Burlingame team wore "dainty white" and with more pony reserves put on a good show. At the end of the match the tie score four to four required an extended period of play. C. E. Maud with an excellent shot won the match. Old polo players who witnessed the game declared it was one of the most scientifically and perfectly played matches of any they had seen. C. E. Maud and R. L. Bettner were considered among the finest players in the state. The Burlingame boys in spite of losing were good sports and the newspapers praised their skill and fine riding.[10]

Many of these Riverside polo players were of English or Canadian descent. They came to the area soon after the Riverside Trust Company, Ltd. purchased the Gage Canal and its many acres of land southeast of town. Matthew Gage, an important Riverside land and water developer, in 1890 went to England to complete the sale of the property. As a result there was an influx of British capital and customs which greatly benefited the city.

On June 25, 1897 Riverside Englishmen, their relatives and friends took time out from sports and business to celebrate Queen Victoria's Jubilee. This date marked the 60th anniversary of her accession to the English throne and was not to be overlooked by her Riverside subjects and well-wishers. Planned weeks ahead the celebration consisted of private parties and an elaborate evening at the Opera House which was decorated with roses and palms. Three portraits of Queen Victoria draped with the British flag stood on the stage together with one of President McKinley surrounded by "Old Glory." Some 60 prominent Riversiders of British or Canadian birth sat on the stage facing a filled theatre. Names such as Scarborough, Jarvis, Flowers, Kennedy, Irving, Miller, Skelley, Devine, Milice, Bettner, Gage, McKenzie, McFarland, Lett, and Maud reflected their background.

The program was opened with band music and was followed by that popular quartet of Messrs. Castleman, Hawes, Worsley and Tom Hays

---

9. *Riverside Press and Horticulturist*, Feb. 20, 1897.
10. *Ibid*, Mar. 1, 1897.

Cartoon by Willard Cundiff
from Who's Who in Riverside

P. S. Castleman

singing Scotch songs. Violin and voice solos interspersed speeches by
W. J. McIntyre, A. A. Adair, and H. M. Streeter. George Frost read this
telegram sent to the Queen "The citizens of Riverside, California, British
born and American, send greetings on this the sixtieth anniversary of
Your Majesty's coronation which we celebrate. God save the Queen!
Signed E. F. Kingman—Mayor." Mrs. Priestly Hall then sang the "Star
Spangled Banner." She was vigorously applauded, which showed there
were some Yankees in the audience. Next everyone sang "God Save
the Queen" and in a standing ovation gave three cheers for Queen
Victoria, then three for President McKinley which finished the evening's
celebration.

Well it may have finished the evening's celebration for some but later there were rumors that the Queen had been toasted a little too often that night. The following morning a couple of horses' heads were seen sticking out of some windows in a well-known residence. It seems that three English gentlemen who lived together had celebrated too long but finally made it home on their ponies and by mistake stabled them in their house.[11]

Golf continued to gain in popularity in 1898 and 1899 and the Riverside Polo and Golf Club's course became inadequate for the increasing number of players. In 1898 an active group under Hays' leadership formed the Rubidoux Golf Club. On Eighth Street just east of the Gage Canal he with Arthur Butcher and F. M. Heath laid out their nine hole golf course. Since the land lay above the flow of the canal and there was no water for grass the grounds were oiled. Members built a small shack where players could store their golfing equipment. Semi-yearly tournaments were held with Tom winning the first three matches with Heath a close second.[12]

The Pachappa Golf Club also organized in the fall of 1898, had established a nine hole golf course on an 80 acre site near Victoria and Central avenues just east of Pachappa Hill. Golfers Potts, Skelley, Osburn, P. White, Butcher, and Hewitson helped make the course. Tom Hays, Philip Pedley, C. E. Maude and J. Hewitson were considered the best players. By April, 1899 this course was enlarged to 18 holes and became the best in Riverside. On April 2nd an important local tournament was won by R. Irving with Tom second. Although tournaments were held often and with much enthusiasm it was not until 1900 that ladies were included in tournament play.[13]

The Riverside Polo and Golf Club on March 3rd and 4th, 1899 put on a major southern California golf tournament with the four best players from each of the Los Angeles, Pasadena, and Redlands Clubs competing. By the very slim margin of one stroke Riverside won the match when C. E. Maud beat C. E. Orr of Pasadena who was then considered the area's best player.

On August 4th many of these players returned to Riverside to organize the Southern California Golf Association. Delegates came from six clubs: the Los Angeles Country Club, Redlands Golf Club, Pachappa Golf Club, Pasadena Country Club, Santa Monica Golf Club, and the Riverside Polo and Golf Club. C. E. Maud was elected the first president of the new organization.

On New Year's day 1900 the Rubidoux Golf Club on its 18 hole

11. Information told Carl Conrad in 1927 by George Winterbothan.
12. *Riverside Daily Press: New Century Number,* Dec. 12, 1900.
13. *Ibid.*

course sponsored a very fine golf tournament. Members playing included Girdlestone, Osburn, McNab, Heath, Godfrey, Witherspoon, Howe, H. B. Chase, Harrison, Phelps, Strange, and Tom Hays who won his first major tournament when he beat J. R. McNab in a close game. On the same day the Riverside Polo and Golf Club put on a good program for its members featuring both horse racing and golf. In a long driving golf event C. E. Maud won with W. E. Pedley, second and McNab, third. Adding to the hilarity of the afternoon was a buggy dash won by Charlie Dole, and a cigar-umbrella race. In the latter at the drop of a flag, each man in the race lit a cigar, mounted his horse, opened an umbrella and set out for the goal. J. Harrison Wright won easily with R. Bettner, second.[14]

Tom won his finest golf victory and championship two weeks later on January 15th in the Rubidoux Golf Club finals with a record breaking 27-hole play. His scores for the three rounds were 51, 48, and 50. His closest competitor was H. B. Chase. This performance placed Tom Hays in the front rank of southern California golfers and he was then acknowledged as Riverside's best player.[15]

---

14. *Ibid*, Jan. 2, 1900.
15. *Ibid*, Jan. 15, 1900

CHAPTER VIII

The Great Street Fair at the
Turn of the Century

During the winter of 1899 Riverside had a large orange crop of fine quality; it was the best production to that date. Due to an abundance of water the turn of the century found the city prosperous. In spite of a three-year drought in the county, new wells made it possible to keep the city water rate at 15 cents per inch.[1] The Riverside population figures revealed 7,900 inhabitants, up 70 percent during the last ten years. The city rejoiced that it now had more citizens than San Bernardino's 6,150. According to Bradstreet Riverside had the highest per capita wealth of any city in the United States with its average family worth $12,000, with $1,200 in the bank.[2]

Tom Hays also prospered. He and his wife attended many parties and led a busy social life with his banking and golfing friends. These affairs, held in private homes, usually included progressive whist, euchre, and dancing. The newspaper invariably reported the details of such events the following day. As their Sixth Street house soon proved too small they moved in the summer of 1896 into a beautiful large home at the corner of Cridge and Olivewood avenues. It overlooked the

1. *Riverside Press and Horticulturist*, Jan. 4, 1901.
2. *Ibid*, Apr. 29, 1899.

Courtesy F. Carl Fowler   *The Olivewood House*

Tequesquite Arroyo then planted to olive trees. This house, built by Dr. Frank Moss, was sold to George F. Seger who rented it to Tom. In the spring of 1898 Seger, who was a local real estate agent, needed the house for his growing family. This required the Hays family to move to a cottage on the Glenwood Hotel block, which was their address until the new Glenwood was built in 1902.[3]

There is no evidence that Tom ever lived in a house that he owned. Instead he began in September, 1897 to acquire property, his first purchase being a parcel of three lots costing $200 in the Kendall subdivision near Highgrove. A year later Seger sold him 160 acres in the same area for $525. Onto this property Hays moved from Moreno a house which he hoped to sell.

The years 1897, 1898, and 1899 had been very dry and some Riverside County communities including Moreno, Winchester, and Alessandro had very little water. As a result many houses were moved down Box Springs Grade to a location in Riverside or Highgrove which, thanks to their canal systems, had enough water. James M. Wells, a 13-year employee of the Riverside Light Department, describes how he as a young boy would watch these houses come into town. It was an exciting operation. A house would first be raised on jacks, then heavy planks resting on hardwood rollers were placed underneath and the house lowered on them. A long metal cable would be attached to the house, the other end hooked to a capstan anchored to the ground some distance

3. *Riverside City Directories*, 1898, 1901 and 1902.

down the street. Two horses would be used to wind the cable onto the capstan thus pulling the building down the road. As the house moved men would collect the rollers as they appeared at the rear and hurriedly carry them to the front. When the cable was entirely wound to the capstan it would be unwound, moved down the street, and the procedure repeated. As a good house mover could move a house about two blocks an hour the trip from Moreno would take several days.[4] After thus improving his property with a house Tom sold it and reinvested in West Eighth Street lots.

As M. J. Daniels, the bank's president, became very ill with rheumatism in the spring of 1898, Hays for four months had to assume most of Daniels' work.[5] This was done so efficiently that, even after Daniels

George E. Bittenger   Judge J. S. Noyes

returned to work, he left additional responsibilities to Tom while he spent more time on politics. In July, 1898 Hays announced for the bank a paid up capital and surplus of $85,000 in gold and claimed the largest volume of business in Riverside County.

The previous year Daniels had been sent to Washington, D.C., to work for the passage of the Dingley Citrus Tariff which would put an

4. Interviews with James M. Wells, 1971.
5. *Riverside Daily Press*, April 1, 1898.

Riverside Municipal Museum Collection   *Riverside County Hospital*

import duty of one cent a pound on citrus from Europe. Riverside growers felt this would be of great benefit to them. After the successful passage of the tariff Daniels was soon mentioned as a possible United States Congressman. The newspaper noted, "He is a successful fruit grower on a large scale and president of the Orange Growers Bank. His public and private life is clean." In August, 1898 Daniels was endorsed as a congressional candidate by the Republican convention meeting at the Y.M.C.A. Tom played an important part in Daniels' nomination and worked hard for his. 1902 election.

In the 1900 spring primary election Hays campaigned successfully for Superior Court Judge Joseph S. Noyes. First elected to this position in 1893, Noyes had become a controversial judge having had a number of important decisions overruled by higher courts. The following August when the Riverside County Republican Convention met, Tom Hays was elected president and I. S. Logan, secretary of the newly formed Republican County Central Committee. This group endorsed William McKinley for President, Theodore Roosevelt for Vice-President, and Judge Noyes for re-election. McKinley and Roosevelt easily won in November but the local campaign was hard and bitter for Noyes. He was re-elected, however, over his opponent, John G. North, in spite of opposition by the *Riverside Daily Press*.[6]

6. *Riverside Press and Horticulturist*, Aug. 24, 1900.

In addition to his political and real estate activities Tom on February 3, 1900 joined some Riverside men in the incorporation of the Aetna Oil Company. Directors were J. R. Johnston, president; S. Masters, vice-president; R. W. A. Godfrey, treasurer; Shirley C. Ward, director; and Tom Hays, secretary. The company, capitalized at $640,000, owned 640 acres of oil land in north Bakersfield. After fighting and winning a court case against the scrippers and mineral locators (J. R. Johnston vs. Conklin) the company in July won a clear title to its land then valued at two million dollars. This was the period of the oil boom in Bakersfield. Various Riverside men including W. G. Fraser, G. E. Bittinger, W. S. Collins, N. C. Younglove and H. W. Bordwell became involved in this new business. Some of them made considerable money.

Other signs of city prosperity included the electrification of the street car line, improvements in streets and parks, and a small building boom. Riverside people, since the formal opening on April 14, 1899 of their new electric street car line, were able to ride the four new trolley cars from Sixth and Main to Van Buren Avenue in Arlington. Later the line was extended to First Street and then to Fairmount Park. This park under the direction and hard work of Captain C. M. Dexter had grown during the last three years to be a favorite picnic spot shaded by memorial trees. On October 12, 1897 the local Grand Army of the Republic requested permission to hold a reunion and barbecue on the city-owned lands northwest of town. After granting the request the city trustees dedicated 35 acres of land to public use, thus establishing Fairmount Park.[7]

In March, 1900 a $20,000 Riverside County Hospital was under construction on a 70-acre site at Magnolia and Harrison streets.[8] A very severe earthquake which occurred early Christmas morning of 1899 had almost totally destroyed the former county hospital located in San Jacinto. That city, together with Hemet, Winchester, and Temecula, suffered extensive damage to its buildings and roads. Old Tahquitz Peak in the San Jacinto Mountains was said to have rumbled, roared, and smoked, giving credence to the Indian belief that the cannibal god Tahquitz lived within. The county supervisors fearful of other earthquakes voted immediately to relocate the hospital to Riverside.

This large building, designed and constructed by local architect A. W. Boggs, used brick and window frames from the old destroyed hospital. It was probably Riverside's first structure to be built in the new Mission Revival style and was followed on October 25, 1900 by the cornerstone

7. *Ibid*, Oct. 9, 1897.
8. *Ibid*, Mar. 10, 1900.

laying of the First Church of Christ Scientist, which set the style for many more buildings in this unusual design.

While many small business blocks or quality homes were planned or under construction, the biggest building to be recently completed was the $25,000 George N. Reynolds Department Store on the northeast corner of Main and Ninth streets. Coming to Riverside in 1885 George Reynolds opened a small store in the Dyer Block which had just been built. Starting with little capital and a small stock of clothing, hats, and shoes, his business grew rapidly. After a year he moved to the Castleman Block where he remained until 1896. That year he built and occupied the Reynolds Block on the east side of Main Street between Seventh and Eighth, but within three years this structure was inadequate.[9]

By April 5, 1900 the new larger store built on the northeast corner of Main and Ninth was finished and a formal opening permitted the viewing of Riverside's finest department store. A candy shop and soda fountain occupied the north front; elegant ladies' hats were sold on the south front, while the rest of the main floor displayed clothing, books, and stationery. Two elevators took customers to the second, third, and basement floors. Carpets, drugs, and wallpapers were on the second floor, and toys, a candy kitchen, and work area on the third. In the basement George T. Mott sold hardware and bicycle equipment.

One week after the new store opened, Riverside marked her prosperity with an eight day "Street Fair and Water Plentitude Celebration" running from Saturday the 14th to the 21st of April. Frank Miller, after meeting L. W. Buckley who was a Glenwood visitor that had managed the Irish Fair in San Francisco, took the idea of a fair to the city trustees. They hired Buckley as manager and appointed George Frost as chairman. Serving as an executive committee were 19 chairmen of sectional committees, including Mrs. L. F. Darling, Ladies Department; C. H. Low, citrus exhibits; A. S. White, awards; Frank Miller, attractions; R. L. Bettner, sports; H. H. Monroe, press and advertising; F. A. Tetley, Fireman's Day; J. A. Simms, street decorations; and Tom Hays, finance.[10]

For many days before the fair opened merchants, companies, and societies were busy building the 65 booths that lined Main Street from Sixth to Tenth. Green, gold, and white banners gaily fluttered overhead when the fair opened with a brief ceremony Saturday morning. The booths, according to the Los Angeles Times, "resembled little palaces in fairyland, many having touches of Oriental splendor." The Reynolds store booth featured the history of Riverside's navel orange with Luther

9. Ibid, Apr. 7, 1900.
10. Ibid, Mar. 10, 1900.

Bordwell Photo   *Tibbets Booth at the Fair*

Tibbets dispensing verbal and printed matter. He and his wife Eliza (deceased 1898) had been responsible for the local introduction of the navel orange in 1873. A big sign across the booth's top read "$21,025,490 brought into Riverside by its oranges in 18 years. Mr. Luther C. Tibbits who occupies this booth planted the first budded Washington orange tree in the world."[11]

To anyone who would listen Tibbets told how he came to Riverside in December, 1870 when there was only one house in town. Built as a home and colony office this building stood on the site of the present Santa Fe depot. Tibbets said that in 1872 he took up a government homestead just south of town and built a small house. In 1873 his wife Eliza arrived from Washington, D.C., where she had known William Saunders, Superintendent of Gardens and Grounds for the U.S. Department of Agriculture. According to Tibbets, at the request of his wife Eliza, Saunders mailed to them two small navel orange trees. Packed bare-root in moss they arrived by mail in Riverside about December 10, 1873, after being a month on the way. First fruiting in 1875 they would revolutionize the local citrus industry. The first buds taken from these trees were obtained by Messrs. Cover and McCoy who rebudded their

---

11. Name misspelled in the sign as Tibbits, not Tibbets.

near-by orchard to this delicious orange.[12]

What Tibbets did not realize was that the week that he spent occupying the street fair booth would be his last public appearance. Born in June, 1820 he was now 80 years old and in failing health. Soon he was to move in with Mrs. Ruth Archer who had been Mrs. Tibbets' close friend. Mrs. Archer took care of him for some months but on September 5, 1901 she suffered a stroke and entered the new Riverside County Hospital. Tibbets at that time was taken to the same hospital where he was kept comfortable until his death on July 21, 1902. Before Tibbets died H. H. Monroe, a newspaperman working with the *Riverside Daily Press*, undertook a drive for funds for Tibbets' behalf but raised only $150. Riversiders did not respond to the plea, apparently feeling that Tibbets with his many cantankerous law suits had been improvident.[13]

Other unusual booths at the street fair included that of Sebrell's Drug Store which exhibited a big mortar and pestle from which gushing soda pop was sold by pretty girls. Alguires' booth displayed agricultural equipment and a buggy with pneumatic rubber tires. A wonderful assortment of Chinese and Japanese curios, which were all for sale, lined the booth of the Gem Bazaar. Hemet's display was decorated with its produce, including citrus, olive oil, potatoes, broom corn, and all kinds of dried fruit and nuts. Photographer S. P. Tresslar's camera exhibit and scenic views of the fair attracted much attention. The mission-style booth of G. Rouse and Company won the $50 first prize award showing store merchandise tastefully arranged by Charlie Rouse who did that store's artistic displays. Other booths and side show exhibits included agricultural displays, fortune tellers, Tally's Edison Projectoscope showing moving pictures of the battle of Manila,[14] the huge animated rubber man moved by steam, Ragtime Cakewalkers, and other marvels.

A large tent at Seventh and Main housed the exhibit of the Twenty-eighth Agricultural District featuring citrus fruits and colorful citrus labels of the many local packinghouses. Included in the same tent were fine Belgian hares then grown for profit as a Riverside County industry.

The Womens' Building, in the old Reynolds store, displayed fancy needlework, quilts, jams, jellies, and other kinds of artistic products. First prize in the art work and oil painting was won by Mamie Roe, local artist.

William Elliott in his booth sold Elliotta Mineral Springs Water which was proclaimed for its health giving and effervescent qualities.

12. *Riverside Enterprise*, April 20, 1900.
13. *Riverside Daily Press*, July 21, 1902.
    and Klotz, Lawton, Hall. *History of Citrus in Riverside Area* (Museum Press, 1969).
14. This is the first mention that the author found of motion pictures shown in Riverside.

Riverside Municipal Museum Collection   *The start of the parade,*
New Burt Block on the left.

In February, 1898 Elliott when digging a well on his ranch a half mile north of town had struck warm mineral water. As a result the following May he opened a new "swimming bath", enclosed it with a building, and called it the Elliotta Plunge and Mineral Springs.[15] Located on Strong between Main and Orange streets it became a popular swimming resort and picnic area. The sulphur water of the spring was also aerated, bottled, and sold.

One of the best exhibits of the fair was a miniature reproduction of Riverside's water system which showed mountains, valleys, streams, wells, canals, a mill, orchards, domestic animals, houses, and fields with water flowing through this landscape. The Riverside Water Company did most of the design and installation work.

On the first day in an exhibition polo match the Riverside team of J. Harrison Wright, C. E. Maud, G. L. Waring and Charlie Dole won 8 to 1 over the Santa Barbara four. Dole played an excellent game making three of the eight scores. Monday a large crowd saw horse racing sponsored by the Riverside Fair and Driving Association at the Riverside Gentleman's Driving Park. This 17 acre park formerly known as Hall's Race Track had been purchased the preceding February by the newly incorporated association which improved it and built new buildings.[16]

15. *Riverside Press and Horticulturist*, May 28, 1898.
16. *Ibid*, Feb. 24, 1900.

Leaders of this group were L. A. Witherspoon, G. W. Dixson, and R. L. Bettner who with other racing enthusiasts used the track weekly and staged races for the fair visitors. Los Angeles sent some fast horses and won some prizes. The last race of the day was widely advertised as southern California's first auto race but only W. S. Collins and his two seated car appeared. It raced alone, making a mile in 3.05 minutes and receiving an enthusiastic response from the crowd.

Tuesday was called Los Angeles Chamber of Commerce Day and Fireman's Day. After a parade featuring the Los Angeles and San Diego hook and ladder companies with their beautiful equipment, the fire company teams of San Bernardino, Redlands, Elsinore, and Riverside competed in a display of skill. Riverside was very proud of its "fire laddies." In September, 1898 they had occupied their first fire station which was built for them by J. A. Simms and leased by the city for $45 a month. Located on Seventh Street west of the Loring Block, the brick building of two floors housed the horse-drawn fire and hook and ladder wagons.[17] The boys' training and skill had improved with the new equipment.

This was demonstrated when Riverside's Hose Company No. 2 won over the San Bernardino and Redlands teams in a contest at the fair. In this competition the men ran 300 feet with a hose reel, attached the hose to a hydrant, then laid out 150 feet of hose and turned on the water. When water emerged from the hose, time was called. Redlands lost its nozzle on a first try and on a second got a bad leak in its connection and gave up. Riverside's running time was 40 seconds. Riverside lost to San Bernardino in a race where seven firemen ran 300 feet with a long ladder, raised it against a building, and climbed to the top. A final event at Eighth and Lime streets was raising the ladder 75 feet into the air against the courthouse and wetting down the big roof. They also wet down the near-by spectators.[18]

Nightly, Papinta, queen of mirror and fire dancers, with her interocean vaudeville stars, performed to full houses at the Loring Opera. Free street shows included the High Diving Dog, Leon's and Lolita's flying trapeze act, and Guin's famous Parisian tightrope walking and juggling show. Some days crowds were so large that not enough hotel rooms were available, requiring people to sleep on the street or take the special trains to Los Angeles or San Bernardino hotels.

Tuesday and Wednesday the Southern California Woman's Parliament held its annual meeting in Riverside as a feature of the fair. Thurs-

17. *Ibid*, Sept. 3, 1898.
18. *Ibid*, April 12, 1900.

Bordwell Photo   *Booth at Main and Eighth Streets*

day professional and amateur bicycle races were run on the Wheelmen's Saucer Track, but Friday was the biggest day of all with the floral parade, baby show, baby coach, and children's parades.

The floral parade was led by floats carrying officials of the fair, followed by the Perris Indian School Band.[19] Then came decorated coaches, horses, tallyhos, floats, firemen's rigs, 35 bicycles, and school children. The Rathbone Sisters, an auxiliary of the Knights of Pythias, won the tallyho award with its yellow roses and beautifully dressed women. It was generally agreed, however, that the Rubidoux Club's tallyho, which did not compete for the prize, surpassed everything in elegance. Carrying 14 club members dressed in black suits, white boutonnieres and white straw hats, the black tallyho with its six white horses made a striking exhibit. Six other club members, three and three to a side, on beautiful horses wore rich colonial liveries complete with powdered wigs and tricorn hats. Tom Hays sat on the front seat of the tallyho with Gaylor Rouse and Harry Chase.[20]

Henry and Bob Hamilton of Cahuilla won all the prizes for the best decorated and most beautiful horses. Miss Doris Heap won first prize for her lovely carriage and the San Diego Hook and Ladder Company took the highest award for its fine flower-decked fire wagon.

19. Predecessor of Sherman Institute.
20. *Riverside Enterprise*, April 20, 1900.

The baby show included 80 babies of all nationalities. Mrs. Tom Hays presented many prizes to the babies and children winning in the various categories: the most unique baby was an attractive Chinese boy, Robee Fay; best Highland laddie and lassie, James and Cecila Irving; best soldier, Frank Brown; best flower girl, Dorothea Bettner; and prettiest colored baby, Helen Blanton. Special awards went to Charlie Reynolds as Uncle Sam, Dorothy Seger as the Goddess of Liberty, and Percy Gilliland, best baby in decorated coach.

Friday night it rained and Saturday the bicycle races were canceled due to the mud. The bunting hung limp and the street carnival faded when the merchants began dismantling their booths. The fair was ended but never in the history of Riverside had so many people had so much fun. The event was more successful than the most sanguine expected and for months continued as the chief topic of conversation. The newspaper pointed out that the successful street fair gave striking evidence of Riverside's wave of prosperity. During a period of serious drought in southern California, Riverside's thirty square miles of orange groves had yielded that season over 3,000 carloads of oranges. Three great canals running full of water had made this possible.[21] In spite of this success, Tom, as chairman of finance, had to appear before the city trustees and request $900. The committee had spent too much when they guaranteed the expenses of the exhibiting Los Angeles Firemen.

When the Riverside Elks Club organized on February 2, 1901, the city had another kind of celebration. Some 275 Elks, which included out-of-town visitors and new local members, met at the Odd Fellows Hall for their first meeting. Tom Hays was the newly elected Exalted Ruler; B. F. Coons, Esteemed Leading Knight; and Frank D. Lewis, Esteemed Royal Knight of the new chapter 643, B.P.O.E. Over the officers' chairs hung a beautiful elk's head loaned by M. E. Taber.

After the meeting everyone enjoyed an elaborate banquet served in Armory Hall located three blocks north of the Odd Fellows Block on Main Street. The menu included oyster cocktails, hot and cold roasts, lobster and chicken salads, desserts, a variety of wines, and ended with Mumm's champagne, cigars, and coffee. The dinner finished in a very gay mood at a very late hour. The following Sunday nine ministers of Riverside churches protested in their sermons the "Bacchanalian revel" held by the Elks Club. Some said that among guests from Los Angeles "29 represented the liquor interests who brought cases of hard liquor and beer which flowed freely all that evening." Various church congregations

---

21. *Riverside Press and Horticulturist*, May 5, 1900.

agreeing with the ministers, stood in protest against such free use of alcoholic drinks. The Baptist minister said he hoped to ask Carrie Nation to visit Riverside.[22] With her hatchet she had just finished saloon-wrecking expeditions in Chicago and Topeka, Kansas, and warned those cities to clean things up or she would be back. It would have been difficult, however, for her to have visited Riverside because at that moment she was in jail, after refusing to post bail for malicious destruction of property.[23] In any case things soon quieted down for the new Elks Club. The next news item tells how the club organized its members into two baseball teams with Tom Hays and F. D. Lewis as captains.

ELLIOTTA MINERAL SPRINGS

AND PLUNGE BATH

---

22. *Ibid*, Feb. 12, 1901.
23. *Ibid*, Feb. 22, 1901.

PROGRAM

INTERMISSION.

Intermezzo—"Naila".....................Theo. Moses
Orchestra.

PAPINTA,

The Enchanting Myriad Dancer, in the most beautiful spectacular dances that human skill has ever produced.

1. Danse La Bonlevard.   2. Danse Du Diable.
3. Danse La Volcano.   4. Danse Du Jardiniere.

THE MICHELSONS,

America's Foremost Banjoists.

W. C. FIELD'S,

The Wonderful Eccentric Juggler, (Direct from the Folies Bergeres, Paris).

Wait for the Prince of Palmist,
ASHER, The Great.

NOTE—There will be matinee performances each afternoon at 2:15, when the entire bill will be rendered.

Matinee special prices—Any seat down stairs, 50c ; balcony, 25c Gallery, 10c.

Loring Opera House Company.

(INCORPORATED)
FRANK A. MILLER, Secretary and Manager
S. C. EVANS, President
W. A. HAYT, Vice-Pres. A. S. WHITE, Treas.
J. G. NORTH   J. A. SIMMS   L. C. WAITE

House Prices

Orchestra—Rows A B C and D	$ .75
Parquet—E to M inclusive	1.00
Parquet Circle—N O and P	.75
Loges—each seat	1.25
Box—each seat	1.50
Dress Circle—Balcony	.50
Gallery—Ticket Office on west side	.25

The management respectfully requests ladies whose hats are of dimensions likely to obstruct the view, to remove them while in the theatre, as those seated back of them are entitled to an unobstructed sight of the stage.

The box-sheet will be placed on display at the O era House Drug Store at 10 a. m. three days before each attraction, and remain open day and evening until 7 p. m. the day of the attraction.

While we dote on babies—the dear little things—they are very much better off in the nursery than at the theatre—where people have paid to attend the evening performances will begin not later than 8:15, and patrons are requested not to disturb the audience by late coming.

Parties desiring cab or carriage during inclement weather, will find call by applying at the box-office.

Hotel Arcadia, Santa Monica

CHAPTER IX

Frank Miller, Another Man About Town

Although he worked closely with Hays on many civic or club projects Frank Miller was ten years older and much superior to Tom in real concern about the city's development. One has the feeling after close reading of the old newspaprs that Hays was not interested in street paving, tree planting, park development, and commercial building. Miller, in contrast, was a leader promoting all of them.

Tom came to Riverside in 1890 when he was 23 years old but Miller had first come as a boy of 16 years when his father Christopher Columbus Miller arrived in 1874 to work on Riverside's canals. Frank had helped his father build a ten room adobe house on the city block bounded by Main, Seventh, Orange,and Sixth streets. This block was given to Frank's father in lieu of $375 of back wages due him from the Southern California Colony Association which had founded the city.[1]

Frank, a serious hardworking young man, soon went into business for himself, acquiring 20 acres of land south of town, raising and selling seed potatoes, and planting citrus. In an 1879 trce survey he was listed as owning 1,500 orange and 240 lime trees. In October of that year he built a brick building on Main Street and began operating his Blue Front Grocery Store.

A Swedish engineer G. O. Newman, who worked with C. C. Miller,

1. Zona Gale, *Frank Miller of Mission Inn*, (New York, 1939) p. 38.

in 1876 married Miller's oldest daughter Emma. Two *months* ~~years~~ later A. S. White, a wealthy man from New York, moved into the adobe as Miller's first paying guest. In December, 1878 C. C. Miller and Newman, his son-in-law, built a large addition to the Glenwood Cottage. Of wood frame construction two stories high, it was attached to the north side of the adobe home and provided a spacious dining room, office, kitchen, a large cellar, and a row of bed chambers. This enabled them to take in more guests. Thus C. C. Miller founded the hotel that was to become so important under his son's ownership.[2]

A. S. White
Courtesy Donald D. Miller

In February, 1880 Frank Miller, having sold his orange grove, paid his father $5,000 for the block of land with the family home and the addition. His father then resumed his engineering work on the Blythe Canal. Four months later Dr. Craig's Hotel, which was an 1871 landmark built on the corner across Orange Street from the Glenwood, burnt to the ground. As a result of the lessened competition Miller's hotel business improved. The first thing Miller did after acquiring the hotel was to landscape the grounds and plant pepper trees all around his block.

---

2. *Riverside Daily Press*, Dec. 21, 1878.

Hotels.

HOTEL GLENWOOD,
RIVERSIDE.

The Popular Resort in Southern California for Pleasure and Health.

Fine Drives! Beautiful Orange Groves! Magnificent Scenery!

THE VISITOR TO RIVERSIDE WILL FIND THIS ONE OF THE BEST AND MOST COMFORT-able resorts in Southern California. It is surrounded by two and one-half acres of orange and other fruit trees, shrubbery and lawns, a quarter of a mile of broad verandas, glazed in, vine sheltered or open sunshine, as may be preferred for promenade Plenty of sunny rooms with opportunity for fires and electric bell service. Hotel supplied with the PUREST SPRING WATER.

This Property for Sale at a Bargain.

F. W. RICHARDSON, **FRANK A. MILLER,**
n9w46tf-2 **Manager.** **Proprietor.**

In 1882 he built, at a cost of $10,000, a large 54 by 134 foot wooden, two-storied, plain addition to his hotel. It was attached to the west side of the adobe home, extending towards Main Street and adding thirty new guest rooms with openings onto side porches.[3]

Also in 1882 Miller leased the Park Boarding House near the city park, furnished it, and for five years operated it without a dining room. Now an experienced hotel man, he was asked in July, 1884 to decorate and furnish the new Long Beach Hotel. The work finished, he remained to open the hotel to the public and run a very busy place for the summer season.

That same year he sold his Blue Front Store and built on the rear of his hotel block facing Orange Street a large roller skating rink. It proved a very popular place, frequently being filled to capacity especially during the evenings. The newspaper called it "a bottled up thunder storm."

The early years being difficult, Miller from 1885 to 1887 tried to sell his hotel by advertising that it had "two and a half acres, a skating rink, a bowling alley, billiard tables, comfortable rooms, an excellent kitchen, and a Concord coach which met all trains." This coach was driven by his brother Ed E. Miller who was experienced with horses. Although called a wonderful bargain in the advertisement, the hotel failed to sell.[4]

In 1885 Miller leased the Glenwood Cottages, as his hotel was then called, to his sister Alice and her husband, Frank W. Richardson. For many years she had ably assisted her brother in the management. For almost three years Miller and his wife Isabella managed the Hotel

3. *Riverside Press and Horticulturist*, Feb. 4, 1882.
4. *Ibid*, June 18, 1885.

Palomares in Pomona. When this hotel was greatly enlarged in 1887, he took a new job as agent to organize and develop the boom town of Claremont for the Pacific Land Improvement Company.[5] In late 1887 the big real estate boom began to fade and he returned to Riverside to help organize the building of the Loring Block and carry on his many other activities.

A few years earlier Frank Miller had formed a real estate partnership with his long time friend, A. S. White. When the Loring Block was

Walter Raymond   *Frank A. Miller, 1896*

finished they moved their real estate office into the corner room of the main floor. They were the agents for the corporation which owned the building and for 16 years Miller also had the responsibility of managing its opera productions.

In 1888 the Glenwood acquired a new ladies' parlor, a larger office, and the size of the dining room was doubled so that it could seat 160 guests. Contractor Charles T. Rice did the work for $3,000. Also, two years earlier some individual cottages were constructed on the east side of the hotel block. Except for some minor alterations the Glenwood existed basically as described until 1902.

With W. A. Hayt, Miller in 1886 was one of the founders of the horse-drawn trolley line and while managing it in 1898 electrified and

5. Esther Klotz. "Pomona's Palomares Hotel." (Pomona Valley Historian, 1970).

enlarged the system.[6] In 1887 he gave some land on his block so that a large three-storied Y.M.C.A. could be built facing Main Street. All his life he also worked with the Congregational Church promoting its activities and assisting in the construction of its churches. He went into politics in order to help bring about the formation in 1893 of the new County of Riverside. He knew well that what helped the city also helped his growing hotel.

Frank Miller's fame as a hotel man began to spread, for he knew how to keep his guests comfortable and entertained. Since many of them came on the Raymond-Whitcomb Tours Miller and Walter Raymond became good friends. Raymond owned a huge Pasadena hotel and another one in Glenwood Springs, Colorado, which then was a popular resort. Called the Colorado Hotel it was the most splendid of all the ten hotels that Frank Miller saw in June, 1894 when he made a trip to Colorado. Earlier that year, as he expected to build a new hotel, he had incorporated the Glenwood with nine local directors.[7] Unfortunately, after returning from the Hotel Colorado with its architectural plans he was unable to secure the necessary capital and had to postpone the construction.

When the Hotel Raymond burnt in 1895 the insurance company asked Miller to evaluate the furnishings as he was considered one of the most knowledgeable of the local hotel men. In 1896 he was made president of the Southern California Hotel Men's Association and had much to do with the organizing and planning of a trip to California that year for the Hotel Men's Mutual Benefit Association. This nationwide hotel group, accompanied by their wives or relatives, spent 16 days in California during April attending their annual convention and sightseeing. Miller's organization acted as host. In a book entitled *The H.M.M.B.A. in California*, G. Wharton James described their trip to the scenic spots and important hotels. The Glenwood Tavern, then managed by F. W. Richardson and wife, was one of their overnight stops. James called it a cozy homelike place, rather old and quaint.

Miller made another attempt to build in 1897 and 1898 when the Riverside County Board of Supervisors accepted his plans for a new hotel and courthouse building. In May, 1897 the supervisors placed an ad in the *Riverside Enterprise* asking for rental or purchase bids for new courthouse space. The courthouse, then occupying the first floor of the Arlington Hotel at Eighth and Lime streets, was considered inadequate and a fire trap. The various proposals made included an offer to sell the

---

6. *Riverside Press and Horticulturist*, Aug. 6, 1898.
7. *Riverside Press and Horticulturist*, June 9, 1894.

Rowell Hotel and adjoining land for $45,000, sale of various land sites for a new building, and Frank Miller's plan for a joint courthouse and hotel to be built on his block.

On July 6, 1897 Miller appeared before the Board of Supervisors and offered to build a 200 room hotel and a courthouse wing of two floors having 16 rooms, three fire-proof vaults, and on the second floor a 35 by 36 foot courtroom. Miller displayed plans drawn by the well known Los Angeles architectural firm of Eisen and Hunt.[8] At that time Sumner P. Hunt was the leading authority on Mission Revival architecture.

Attached to Miller's new hotel the courthouse would form the building's west wing which would front 80 feet on Main Street at Seventh. It would be leased to the County of Riverside at $350 a month for a five year period subject to renewal on the same terms. At the board meeting of August 11th Supervisor Fred Dunbar moved acceptance of Miller's proposal and the resolution passed. On August 24th the contract was signed with only Supervisor J. M. Edmiston refusing. He declared he preferred that the county own its own building and that it should build at once. With Supervisor H. C. Thompson absent the vote was three to one in favor of Miller's proposal with John Shaver, Fred Dunbar, and A. Compton voting yes. Miller posted bond for $5,000 to complete the courthouse wing by June 1, 1898 and install marble wash basins, speaking tubes, heating, and other modern conveniences in all offices. The *Los Angeles Times* (August 28, 1897) pictured the new building covering the entire block with a 150 by 200 foot center courtyard. The newspaper stated that the lease had been signed and that Frank Miller was away making financial arrangements.

Again Miller had difficulty financing his project and on March 23, 1898 he appeared before the supervisors requesting more time. No start had been made on the construction. Later, after considerable deliberation, the supervisors announced that they had entered into a three-way contract with Frank Miller and H. B. Everest, owner of the Arlington Hotel, who at that time held the courthouse lease. Miller would have until July 1, 1898 to begin construction of the new courthouse wing. If the building was started at that date the time for occupancy would be extended. If no construction was under way the county would release Miller from his bond and accept Everest's proposal of the lease of his entire hotel for five years at $300 a month.

After December, 1897 no further notice of Miller's proposal ap-

---

8. *Minutes*, Riverside County Board of Supervisors.

Riverside Public Library

peared in the newspapers, but on December 4th another announcement revealed that he had leased the big Hotel Arcadia in Santa Monica which overlooked the ocean. During the next two years, while his sister Alice and husband F. W. Richardson ran the Glenwood, Miller did an excellent job managing the Arcadia Hotel, landscaping the grounds, and keeping his guests happy. Under his direction the hotel became very popular. The idea of a new hotel in Riverside faded and on July 1, 1898 the proposed five year lease of the entire Arlington Hotel as the courthouse became effective.[9]

In the fall of 1901 Miller was working with the Riverside Chamber of Commerce when Tom Hays was made president. A new board of 17 important businessmen adopted a revised set of bylaws. They assumed the debts of the original Chamber of Commerce which from its formation in 1897 had been rather inactive under the presidency of George Frost.[10]

The organization immediately agreed to work on two projects. The first was to welcome and cooperate with the San Pedro, Los Angeles, and Salt Lake Railroad Company which was soon to lay a new line through Riverside. In January, 1901 the company bought the Los Angeles Terminal Railroad and the San Pedro Harbor and Los Angeles Terminal Land Company for $2,500,000 which gave it a railway from San Pedro to Los Angeles. In March, 1901 the company incorporated with U.S.

9. *Minutes,* Riverside County Board of Supervisors.
10. *Riverside Press and Horticulturist,* Oct. 18, 1901.

Senator W. A. Clark of Butte, Montana, as president. During the first year track was laid from Los Angeles to Pomona and other construction was under way near Salt Lake City, the terminus. The railroad needed to acquire property and a right-of-way through Riverside. In April, 1902 when the railroad applied for a city franchise a committee composed of H. B. Chase, E. S. Multon, W. McBean, G. D. Cunningham, and Tom Hays assured the railroad of local backing.[11]

The second Chamber of Commerce project was the submission in May, 1902 of a new city charter to the Riverside City Board of Trustees. The Chamber of Commerce worked hard for the charter but it was not adopted until 1907 when Samuel C. Evans, Jr. was elected the city's first mayor.

In spite of the excellent work done by Hays during his first year as president discontent with his methods caused some members of the Chamber of Commerce to resign. They declared the organization was being used to further Hays' political activity. Other members also wondered where Tom obtained all the money he was spending. Nevertheless, he did much to "boom the city" by making speeches, and publishing booklets on picturesque Riverside pointing out its many new buildings under construction.

One such building was the Riverside Public Library. Largely as a result of the activity of the Riverside Woman's Club, Dr. G. H. Deere, and Lyman Evans, the city in September, 1901 received a $20,000 Carnegie grant to build a library. Building contractor J. W. Carroll, using plans drawn by Los Angeles Architects Burnham and Bliesner started construction in April, 1902 on the northeast corner of Seventh and Orange.[12] To qualify for the grant the city was required to furnish a suitable site and agree to supply a $2,000 a year budget for maintenance and operation. When opened in August, 1903 the city had an attractive library in Mission Revival style with its interior walls decorated by local artist S. S. Nicolini.

Frank Miller was influential in locating in Riverside the U.S. Government's big Indian school called the Sherman Institute. On July 9, 1901 construction of nine mission-type buildings costing $150,000 was begun by Riverside contractors Boggs, Wilcox and Rose on a 40-acre site at Magnolia and Jackson. James S. Sherman, chairman of the Federal Committee on Indian Affairs, laid the cornerstone of the institute named for him. When the buildings were finished in May, 1902, Indian students

11. *Riverside Press and Horticulturist*, April 25, 1902.
12. *Ibid*, Mar. 11, 1902.

were transferred from the old Perris Indian School near Val Verde into the new buildings.

Miller wanted the institute at this Riverside location because he had just opened the previous April on a site to the north a 23-acre Street Railway Park which was later named Chemawa. He moved the fence and grandstand from the abandoned Athletic Park and built a dance pavilion,

George Reynolds

small lake, an aviary, and a gardener's cottage. With the help of C. M. Loring he planted a variety of trees. The Riverside Polo Club moved to the park and laid out a polo field and a half-mile race track. During the first week a polo game and a three-day cricket match helped celebrate the opening.[13] The park not only added to the city's beauty and pleasure but increased the revenues of the streetcar line managed by Miller.

The city was also improved by the construction in 1901 of a high school on a city block bounded by Lemon, Tenth, Lime, and Ninth streets. The Mission Revival building designed by Long Beach Architect H. F. Starbuck cost $30,000 and was completed in January, 1902.[14] Then the 256 pupils moved from the third floor of the old high school at Fourteenth and Brockton into the new building.

While the school facilities now seemed adequate the city's chief need

13. *Ibid*, April 26, 1901.
14. *Ibid*, Jan. 7, 1902.

Main Street showing the Reynolds store and Reynolds Hotel on the right 1903

was a good modern hotel. On March 25, 1902 the *Press and Horticulturist* announced in headlines that "Tourist Hotels are coming in pairs. George N. Reynolds buys the Casa Palma Hotel and will spend $50,000 on improvements." He planned to rebuild the old 1886 three-storied former Rowell Hotel on Main Street by putting in larger plate glass windows, extending the Ninth Street side to the alley, and joining the two wings. Thus he would make an attractive glassed-enclosed court which would be decorated with tropical plants. The rebuilt structure would have 110 enlarged newly-furnished guest rooms and 13 new bathrooms. Mr. Reynolds asked the city for a bonus subscription of $20,000 and a committee composed of W. G. Fraser, H. B. Chase, George Bittinger, S. C. Evans, Jr., and Tom Hays was appointed to secure the funds.

A few hours after the newspaper received this information Frank Miller sent it a letter stating he was ready to go ahead with his long time plan for construction of a beautiful $150,000 tourist hotel for Riverside. If the citizens would guarantee him a bonus of $25,000 he would build the hotel and have it ready for the 1903 tourist season. He named E. A. Chase, S. C. Evans, Jr., and Charles H. Low as a committee of trustees to receive the money. A corporation would be formed to build and furnish the new hotel, a project in which local people could invest.

For a month, while the citizens wondered what would happen next, nothing new about the project appeared in the newspapers. Who knew what wires were being pulled, what settlements were being made? Finally the announcement came: "Reynolds withdraws, Miller goes ahead." Mr. Reynolds explained his action saying that he feared both bonuses could not be raised even though his committee had pledges of $17,000 to assist him. The remodeling project that he had planned would proceed but on a modified scale and without public funds. It would be done quickly so that the Reynolds Hotel could be open for guests while the new Glenwood was being constructed.

With George Reynold's announcement on April 25, 1902 the way was clear at last, after two unsuccessful attempts, for Frank Miller to build his dream hotel. In less than a year the new Glenwood would be finished, Tom Hays would move his family into an apartment in the east wing, and Riverside would have an outstanding new hotel.

90

Fit the Boys Out for Less than Half

For $1.00 you can buy Boys' Suits that sold for $3.00

We've picked out about 100 suits for boys. Suits at $1.50, $2.00, $2.50 and $3.00, and priced them all at $1.00. The suits picked out are all good grades, but we are broken up on sizes. We don't care to carry broken lines in stock, so we are going to sell these out, and sell them quick, too. Perhaps you don't need one just now, but they are worth buying for fall wear. Come and see them you can't afford to pass them by, when they sell for ....

$1.00

Boys. 50 & 75c Shirts for 39c

Boys shirts, in golf and negligee, odds and ends of line that sold at 50c and 75c. We need the room for our fall line, so have priced them all at, each...... ....

39c

Boys' Wash Suits for 50c that sold as high as $1.98

Odds and ends brought to our notice during inventory. All prices from $1.00 up to $1.98, mostly small sizes, in Russian blouse and Buster Brown effects. Not enough to carry over so we have bunched them in one lot to clear them out at, per suit...... ....

50c

Boys 50c Sweaters for 33c

Boys' cotton sweaters for vacation wear, in all colors and sizes. Regular 50c sweaters, just what the boys like. For this sale, only...... ....

33c

Boys' Corduroy Pants for 39c

Boys' corduroy pants, sizes up to 10 years. Regular 50c values. Strong, well made pants - that won't rip or tear. For this sale, per pair...... ....

39c

The Racket Department Store

BACKSTRAND & GROUT   735 MAIN STREET

The Adobe & Campanile

CHAPTER X

The New Glenwood Hotel

Four days after George Reynolds announced he would not seek a public bonus, Miller put his contractors, A. W. Boggs, Wilcox, and Rose, to work moving the 1878 and 1882 hotel additions to the north side of the block. The latter building was difficult to move, as housemover Thorp found out. But by June 6th he had 60 screwjacks under the large 54 by 134 foot two-storied frame building and very slowly moved it into its new position facing Sixth Street.[1] The other old building was also moved to the rear and fronted on Orange at Sixth Street. Tom Hays, wife, and daughter had been renting a Glenwood Cottage for the last few years. This cottage was moved north, probably with some of their furnishings inside, so that it faced Orange near Sixth Street.

On May 17, 1902 Miller filed with the county clerk the incorporation papers of the Glenwood Hotel Company listing the capitalization at

---

1. *Riverside Press and Horticulturist*, June 6, 1902.

First Church of Christ Scientist

$250,000 with 2,500 shares of common stock at $100. The seven directors were George Frost, president (20 shares); Frank Miller, vice-president and general manager (100 shares); F. W. Richardson, secretary and assistant manager (100 shares); Gaylor Rouse (5 shares), E. A. Chase (5 shares), J. A. Simms (5 shares), and A. S. White (10 shares). Other stockholders were E. E. Miller, brother of Frank (30 shares), G. O. Newman, brother-in-law of Frank (50 shares), and A. P. Johnson (5 shares). These were all the shareholders listed in the incorporation papers still on file in the Riverside County Clerk's office. As these shareholders could raise only $123,000, Miller still had to find double that amount if he were to build and furnish the hotel as planned.

In her book *Frank Miller of the Mission Inn*, Zona Gale states that Henry E. Huntington agreed to invest $75,000 if the public subscribed $25,000.[2] The same committee consisting of S. C. Evans, Jr., W. G. Fraser, George Bittinger, H. B. Chase and Tom Hays, that had worked for Reynolds now worked for Miller and succeeded with the help of others in raising the necessary $25,000.[3]

It is logical to believe that the $100,000 which Miller put into the hotel included the $75,000 promised by Huntington because in January,

---

2. Zona Gale, *Frank Miller of the Mission Inn* (New York, 1938) p. 49.
3. *Riverside Press and Horticulturist*, April 25, 1902.

1903, after the construction was almost finished, a mortgage of $150,000 was voted by the stockholders.[4] In March the Union Trust Company of San Francisco bought the twenty year bonds which yielded eight percent.

A large drawing by Architect Arthur B. Benton appeared in the April 28, 1902 *Press*. Patterned after the Hotel Colorado at Glenwood Springs, the illustration showed a structure with three floors and an attic opening onto a paseo landing. The main building running east and west had two perpendicular wings projecting southward, making a

Frank A. Miller, 1901   *George Frost*

large courtyard decorated with pergolas, open trellises, and tropical plants. No mission dormers, campanile, or remodeled adobe with attached companario bell arch appeared on the original Benton drawing, but would be added by Miller as the hotel was being built.

Arthur B. Benton of Los Angeles was with Sumner Hunt, a consulting architect of the Landmarks Club. In January, 1896 Charles F. Lummis, Benton, and others had founded the club to help restore the fast disintegrating San Fernando, San Juan Capistrano, and other California missions. Benton had spent much time studying mission architecture on which he

4. Riverside County Clerk Records.

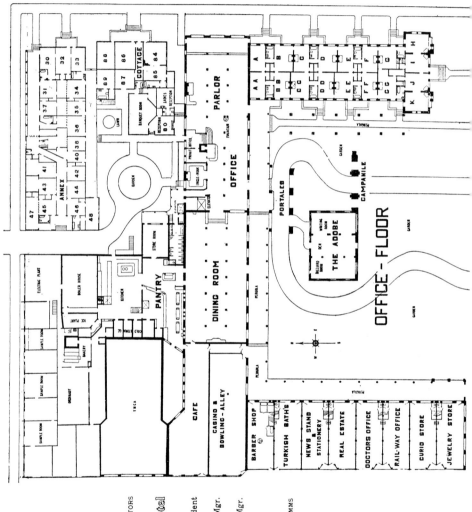

was an authority. Frank Miller, knowing the tourist interest in the romance of the early California missions, used their design in his hotel, but he was never a member of the Landmarks Club. Month after month lists of new members were published by Lummis in his *Sunshine* and *Out West* magazines and Miller's name did not appear.

In October, 1900 the First Church of Christ Scientist, the first Riverside building to be designed by Benton, was under construction with Los Angeles contractor F. L. Spaulding in charge. The design, combining mission and classical details, produced at a cost of $10,470 an elegant church with a seating capacity of 500.[5] It is probable that while this church was under construction Benton stayed at the Glenwood and listened to Frank Miller's plans for a new hotel.

On June 13, 1902 the building contracts for the new Glenwood were recorded. Benton's plans and specifications were filed, signed by George Frost, president, and F. W. Richardson, secretary for the Glenwood Hotel Corporation, and by Riverside contractors A. W. Boggs, Wilcox, and Rose. The original contract price was $167,975 but since Miller kept making changes as the building progressed it is hard to say what the final costs totaled.[6] The contract stated all work was to be finished by January 1, 1903 with a premium to be paid if the work was completed sooner. Heavy rains, however, prevented this.

By August the heavy foundations of the hotel were laid and the workers were soon putting up the framework. Walls were of concrete and cement tile with a plastered cement exterior in a rough "pebble-dash" finish. Three large brick firewalls, running from deep in the foundations to above the top floor, divided the building into four sections.[7] In a serious fire of January, 1900 Miller had lost 14 rooms of the old north wing and part of the kitchen. In the middle of the night people had to flee in their negligees. Miller was determined to protect his new hotel.

In the central building on the main floor a large 45 foot wide dining room would front 95 feet on the patio. To the east would be the main lobby with an inglenook fireplace, office, and parlor which opened onto the patio. At the east end of the room a raised platform was planned for the hotel orchestra.

The ground floor of the east wing would have 18 rooms which would be used for the best apartments and Tom and family had reserved four of these. Eight shop rooms in the west wing, which would front on both Main Street and the patio, were to be leased to merchants. North of these stores a bowling alley and a cafe would be constructed next to

5. *Riverside Press and Horticulturist*, Oct. 2, 1900.
6. *Ibid*, June 13, 1902.
7. *Ibid*, Oct. 28 ,1902.

building, the original Miller home located in the center courtyard, was remodeled for billiard, smoking, and lounging rooms.

The new interiors were light, airy and picturesque with their thin curtains over casement windows. Heavy ceiling beams and woodwork stained in a warm brown contrasted with the light plaster walls. In the lobby and dining room little white bell shaped lights, hung by black wrought iron chains, added a sparkle to the rooms at night.

The dining room was especially attractive with a high natural red brick wainscoting topped by a molded wood plate rail on which were

Arthur B. Benton   Henry E. Huntington

displayed antiques, metal platters, and dishes. The brown oak chairs were placed about round tables covered with gleaming white tablecolths. Only the new furniture pieces which Miller and his wife had selected were used to furnish the new hotel.[10] A wide stairway and an elevator took guests to their rooms on the three floors above. On the first mezzanine was a colonial nook with an antique grandfather clock, spinning wheels, and writing desks, all arranged by Albert S. White who made his home at the hotel. On the second mezzanine a Japanese area dedicated to Buddha added an oriental touch.

10. *Ibid*, Oct. 28, 1902.

Riverside Municipal Museum Collection   *Flag Raising at the New Glenwood*

Late in 1902 Tom Hays moved his family into the four beautiful rooms in the east wing that Miller had reserved for them. Later these rooms would be called the Presidential Suite. Situated next to the parlor on the main floor they opened onto both the courtyard and Orange Street. The location was the most desirable and the rooms which were furnished with oriental furniture and Turkish rugs were the finest in the new Glenwood.

Although some building details were unfinished, a Raymond-Whitcomb party of 48 tourists arrived on January 22, 1903 as the first guests of the new hotel. Shown the newly decorated rooms and entertained by the Sherman Institute Band as they dined, the group was enchanted by the comfort and romantic beauty of the place. A new 20-seat horse-drawn Glenwood livery bus built by the Riverside firm of O'Conner and Covey took the guests about the city. This bus, gaily painted orange, green, and yellow, and driven by Glen M. Thompson, met every train.[11]

11. *Riverside Daily Press*, Jan. 8 ,1903.

Gradually the hotel began filling and on January 30th the hotel registered 60 new guests and served 150 people at dinner. The Glenwood Orchestra under the hotel's new musical director, Mr. F. Grover, entertained in the lounge. In charge of the hotel were owner Miller; F. W. Richardson, manager; Alexis Bjornson, host; Miss Minerva Green, cashier; Allis Miller, private correspondent; Ed Miller, head liveryman; and Mrs. F. W. Richardson, buyer. Others were listed as chamber maids and waitresses.

During the afternoon and evening of February 20, 1903 the new Glenwood held a big formal opening. No private invitations were issued. Instead the public was invited to view the completed rooms and grounds. Mr. and Mrs. Frank Miller assisted by the directors of the Glenwood Hotel Corporation and their wives, Architect and Mrs. Arthur B. Benton, and Mrs. James Bettner received the townspeople.

What the local visitors saw was a unique, cloistered, mission-like building enclosing a spacious courtyard filled with palm and pepper trees. They were impressed by the warmth and color of the rooms with fine woodwork, natural brick, open fireplaces, oriental rugs, tables, and comfortable chairs. These were deep-seated arm chairs, cushioned rockers, and adjustable William Morris styles. The effect was subdued luxury. Now Riverside had a beautiful place to enjoy and entertain its guests, and Frank Miller had, after two unsuccessful attempts, completed the first part of his hotel which would become well known throughout the United States and Europe.

Arlington Hotel, Riverside County Courthouse, 1893-1904

CHAPTER XI

Crime Raises its Ugly Head

While all this construction was underway in the area a badly needed county courthouse was being planned. Hays as chairman of the Riverside County Republican Central Committee would have much to say about the construction of this building but first it was necessary to find a site.

In 1897 W. G. Fraser, speaking before the city trustees, pointed out that if the city no longer owned White Park it would reduce city expenses. A city trustee then moved that the city give the park to the county as a location for a new courthouse. Fortunately, three city trustees, E. F. Kingman, Bradford Morse, and S. LaRue voted no, defeating the proposition three to two, thereby saving White Park.[1]

The same year that Frank Miller tried to build a hotel with the courthouse adjoined, Mrs. C. Chalmers, who owned the city block bounded by Main, Tenth, Orange and Eleventh streets, offered to sell to the county her home and block of land for $16,000. Failing to sell the property at that time she sold it in January, 1900 to attorney W. J. McIntyre for $12,500. He said he thought a courthouse would look good at that location.[2]

---

1. *Riverside Press and Horticulturist,* July 17, 1897.
2. *Ibid,* Jan. 19, 1900.

Courtesy Mrs. Thomas Millikin   *Zeno de Moss and Crew*

In March, 1901 the county supervisors advertised for submission of bids for a courthouse site and received the following: W. J. McIntyre, the Chalmers' block, $20,000; Will Lewis, block bounded by Locust, Eleventh, Cedar and Twelfth streets, $3,500; and H. B. Everest, the Arlington Hotel and block, $50,000. Later Everest offered for one dollar to give half of his block if that site were chosen.

For some undisclosed reason W. J. McIntyre sold the Chalmers' block on April 4, 1901 for $20,000 to a well known land speculator, Pliny T. Evans. On that date Tom Hays notarized the deed but at the request of Evans did not record it until July 26, 1901.[3]

On that morning in spite of a motion made by Supervisor John Shaver to defer a decision until their next meeting, Supervisors Fred Dunbar, Edward Lilly, C. W. Craven and A. T. Kimbell voted to buy from Evans for $20,000 Block 10, Range 6, known as the Chalmers' Block. Before the final vote, which was four to one with Shaver voting no, E. W. Holmes and other interested citizens appeared to speak against the purchase. Bradford Morse, city trustee, said the price was excessive and in his opinion a sum of $15,000 to $17,000 was enough. He also

3. Riverside County Deed Records, Book 122, p. 348.

said the $30,000 cost of the jail that the supervisors planned to build on the rear of the Chambers' Block was outrageously expensive especially in view of the fact that the county had only two prisoners at that time.[4] Nevertheless, before long this new facility was under construction with A. W. Boggs as architect.

Earlier the supervisors had set a bond election for the building of the courthouse and after considerable publicity throughout the county the bonds were favorably voted. Plans and specifications were called for and on August 13, 1902 five architectural firms from Los Angeles and Long Beach presented designs in classical, mission, and Italian Renaissance styles. The classical design of Franklin P. Burnham of the Los Angeles architectural firm of Burnham and Bliesner was chosen by the supervisors after a local committee headed by E. A. Chase urged its selection.[5] This was over the protest of Supervisors Dunbar and Craven who preferred a two-storied mission design.

In October submission of construction bids were requested and on November 14th the lowest bid of $137,750 by Los Angeles contractor F. O. Engstrom was accepted. Nine firms, including the Riverside company of Boggs, Wilcox and Rose had bid on the job where only local laborers were to be employed.

Early in December the supervisors decided to alter the courthouse specifications using concrete instead of brick for the foundations, substituting pressed instead of common brick for the steel framed walls, and requiring exterior columns to be of concrete stone rather than brick. Also the steps were to be of granite instead of concrete.

After receiving estimates from Engstrom the supervisors met and voted without discussion to give him $22,530 more for these changes. Loud complaints were heard from other contractors who said $10,000 would have been enough. The *Daily Press* questioned why Tom Hays, M. J. Daniels and others were there conferring with the architect and contractor before the vote of the supervisors. The newspaper stated that evidently collusive agreements had been made earlier. "This star chamber method of transacting public business seems to be a popular system with the supervisors. Taxpayers what do you think?"[6] For $11,640 Frank A. Noyes Jr. offered to supply the different materials needed by the contractor thus saving the county $10,890, but his offer was ignored. A *Press* editorial maintained that materials should have been put out for contractural bid.

Early in the afternoon of May 7, 1903 before the visit of President

---

4. *Riverside Press and Horticulturist*, Mar. 22, 1901.
5. E. A. Chase, *Notebooks*, Vol. I, Riverside Public Library.
6. *Riverside Press and Horticulturist*, Dec. 12, 1902.

Theodore Roosevelt, the courthouse cornerstone was laid with impressive ceremony. Below the cornerstone in a steel box were a copy of Holmes' *History of Riverside County*, lists and photographs of officials and supervisors, a copy of the May 7th *Press*, photographs of the new Glenwood Hotel, Riverside's Water System, scenic town views, and a sprig of the parent navel orange tree.

By the last of July the foundations were finished. The Ionic pillars were rising, the interior common brick walls were going up fast but those of the exterior were delayed by lack of pressed bricks which were in short supply. Zeno DeMoss, the well known local cement contractor, had his men preparing the grounds for the cement walks and steps he would install about the new building. He had won the contract with his low bid of $2,182.

Field Studios   *Tom Hays House*

As an important local politician there is no doubt that Tom Hays had a major part in letting these contracts and he became well acquainted with architects Burnham and Bleisner. On August 14, 1903 after the courthouse was well underway, the newspaper announced that Tom would erect an artistic bungalow on his Rubidoux Hill property.

Hays had first acquired this land from the Dyer estate in the spring of 1902 when he, Robert Bettner, T. H. Dudley, and J. A. Whittier had formed a syndicate and bought it for a real estate development.[7] The property consisted of 24 acres of rock and sagebrush between Fourth and

_____

7. *Riverside Daily Press*, July 19, 1902.

Eighth streets and from Pine to the Santa Ana River. In July of that year William Backus began grading and cutting a 24 foot wide road around the hill called little Mt. Rubidoux. The developers laid out large lots usually 100 by 157 feet in size, placed deed restrictions on future

Elmer W. Holmes
Riverside Public Library Collection

building, and landscaped the area with curbs, trees, and shrubs.[8]

By December an attractive street called Mt. Rubidoux Drive was almost completed and lots were selling very well. The property above the new drive was on the mountain slope and provided an excellent view of the city. In January, 1903 Hays sold five large lots to Charles M. Loring and wife who hoped to build on them. That same month Robert Bettner, who now owned three-fourths of the Rubidoux Heights Tract, sold almost half of it to Tom.[9] Bettner, a prominent real estate man, continued as the tract's sales manager.

The lot on which Hays built his house lay on a lower part of the hill near the west end of Sixth Street and overlooked both the city and the Santa Ana River. Designed by architect Burnham to conform to the rocky site it was constructed with its foundations, wide verandas, and

8. *Ibid.*
9. *Ibid,* Jan. 8, 1903.

fireplace all of "blue marble" stone. A large hallway, reception parlor, and billiard room were finished in oak and so designed that they could be opened to make one large room for entertaining. This house built by contractor A. W. Boggs at a cost of $8,000, was expected to be finished by December, 1903.[10] In November Tom and family were getting ready to move from their "presidential suite" in the Glenwood where they had lived for almost a year. But they were never to occupy their new house because big headlines in the November 16, 1903 *Daily Press* announced, "Hays Has Resigned as Cashier of Bank."

The *Los Angeles Times* broke the story giving the information to the local paper that Tom Hays had been caught in crooked land deals while acting as a Riverside right-of-way agent for the Salt Lake Railroad. For two weeks previously the matter had been hushed up until all the facts were uncovered and the Orange Growers National Bank of Riverside could be informed.

For over a year Tom, using Salt Lake funds, bought property at one price and charged the railroad another. He had been trusted implicitly as he worked with Major J. W. F. Dias, the railroad's right-of-way agent. But two weeks previously in the condemnation suit of the property of Foxton, a Riverside land owner, the railroad's Riverside attorney Wilfred M. Peck discovered that Major Dias had offered $7,000 for a right-of-way that a jury decided was worth only $4,000. Attorney Peck began an intensive investigation of Riverside land deals involving the railroad and discovered the company had been defrauded of more than $8,000 by Hays with Dias' knowledge.[11]

Actually A. S. Halsted, Los Angeles attorney for the railroad, early in September had noted some discrepancies in the matter of right-of-way purchases. He and two of the railroad's vice-presidents, J. Ross Clark and T. E. Gibbon a week earlier met with attorney Peck in his Riverside office. They sent for Hays who reluctantly joined them. When he was confronted with the carefully prepared facts exposing his crookedness he tried to bluff his way out, declaring the funds taken were only "commissions". When faced with exposure and arrest he confessed and deeded to the railroad $12,000 worth of his orange property.[12]

In a later *Los Angeles Times* article entitled "More Hot Stuff on the Salt Lake" T. E. Gibbon explained why Dias was fired by the railroad. Although it was inconclusive that Dias himself had profited there was no doubt that he knew of these frauds which included not only Hays but those of some Riverside real estate agents. It looked now as

10. *Riverside Press and Horticulturist*, Aug. 14, 1903.
11. *Ibid*, Nov. 16, 1903.
12. *Ibid*, Nov. 16, 1903.

if some $60,000 had been lost by the railroad up and down the line, not all of it in Riverside.[13]

Tom's bank, on learning that this shocking news would soon be released, asked for his resignation. This he gave after insisting the bank directors vote him a commendation for "his long and faithful service as cashier on behalf of the stockholders and bank patrons" and noting "that no other officer or stockholder has contributed so much towards the

Gaylor Rouse

financial success and standing of this bank, and that no one has given so freely of his time, talents and ability. Resolved also that he be congratulated, on severing his connection with this bank, that he has been able to show every dollar accounted for, the affairs of his office in order, and his trust well and safely administered." Gaylor Rouse, acting bank president in the absence of President M. J. Daniels, then a Congressman in Washington, D.C., accepted the resignation and announced that M. J. Twogood would succeed Hays as cashier. The bank directors then reluctantly voted to give him the commendation he requested.[14]

The newspaper said Tom's resignation was the result of his Salt Lake operations and did not affect the soundness of the Orange Growers

13. *Los Angeles Times*, Nov. 18, 1903.
14. *Riverside Press and Horticulturist*, Nov. 20, 1903.

National Bank. The whole town, however, was affected. In fact it rocked with the news which for days was the sole topic of conversation. That Tom Hays, the Beau Brummell of Riverside, had confessed that he was a party to such crooked transactions amazed and distressed his many friends and acquaintances. It was unbelievable that this man, a former Chamber of Commerce president, bank cashier, Republican leader, and outstanding club man should be an apparent embezzler. True, lately he had been a high liver and a big spender, a man who never did anything by halves.

After his resignation he declined to make any statement for publication but let it be known he intended to remain in Riverside where he would continue in the real estate business which the newspaper said seemed well adapted to his special talents.

The railroad attorneys, placing little value on the trust deed signed by Hays, immediately issued attachments on his property. They also filed suit against him in the U.S. Circuit Court in Los Angeles, case 1093, San Pedro, Los Angeles, and Salt Lake Railroad vs. H. T. Hays, Defendant, for $8,000 plus interest since October, 1903 and court costs.[15] Tom, considering a counter suit, consulted J. S. Chapman and E. A. Meserve, famous Los Angeles attorneys, and the Riverside law firm of Purington and Adair. On December 17th Tom filed an answer to the railroad's lawsuit against him saying he was innocent of all charges and that he was never an agent for the railroad.

At a quail banquet served to the Elks Club where Tom still presided as their Grand Exalted Ruler, his friends rallied to his support. Mr. Peck, who had uncovered much of the alleged crookedness, was ignored, insulted, and made to feel he was the criminal.[16] The story, however, had not yet ended.

---

15. *Riverside Daily Press*, Nov. 27, 1903.
16. *Riverside Press and Horticulturist*, Nov. 18, 1903.

CHAPTER XII
Tom Goes to Jail

In October, 1902 before Hays ran into difficulties, some of the local socialites and sportsmen formed a new golf and tennis group which they named the Victoria Country Club. Robert L. Bettner, Harry Chase, and Tom Hays in July, 1903 were appointed a committee to find a site on which to lay out the golf and tennis areas and build a clubhouse.[1] The committee selected an 80-acre site located just east of Victoria Hill which the club purchased from the Chase Nursery Company. In the fall of 1903 a rustic two-story clubhouse designed by architect Franklin Burnham was built at the edge of the arroyo overlooking a new nine-hole golf course. The building's exterior of brown oiled wood contrasted with the cream trim, making an attractive clubhouse in an unusual setting.

At its informal opening on February 10, 1904 members were pleased with the wicker and mission oak furniture, the billiard and card rooms, the view of the golf course in the arroyo, and the three fine tennis courts nearby. The first directors of the club were R. L. Bettner, president, and Hubert Hamilton, H. B. Chase, M. J. Twogood, H. R. Green, Frank Miller and F. T. Morrison. Some of these men were close friends of Hays and they together with 43 other businessmen made up the stockholders who subscribed the original $25,000 capital.[2]

Tom, although an original stockholder, never enjoyed the clubhouse which he helped locate. The headlines of November, 1903 stating he had illegally taken money from the Salt Lake Railroad had dampened

1. *Riverside Daily Press*, July 23, 1903.
2. *Ibid*, Oct. 31, 1903.

the enthusiasm of his friends. He missed the opening of the Victoria Clubhouse because he was testifying before the County Grand Jury which later that day indicted him for embezzlement.[3]

On March 12, 1904 Tom gave a party for some Los Angeles friends in his elegant Glenwood apartment to celebrate the arrival in Riverside of the San Pedro, Los Angeles, and Salt Lake Railroad. They opened bottle after bottle of champagne for a very gay evening.[4] Riverside on that same day also put on a real celebration for the arrival of the railroad. At the site of its new mission-style depot on east Seventh Street a flowered gateway had been built through which entered a gaily decorated train bearing railroad and Chamber of Commerce officials. Band music and welcoming speeches entertained the crowd which later that day enjoyed polo, horse racing, and other sports. Railroad vice-president J. Ross Clark told how Riverside would have four trains daily each way. The trip to Los Angeles would take only 55 minutes making it convenient for shoppers. As the line was not finished, there would be a two months wait before one could go to Colton or San Bernardino on the new railroad.

What the speech makers did not explain were the various difficulties the road had experienced such as building the big bridge across the Santa Ana River, the cutting of the roadbed through almost solid rock at the base of Pachappa Mountain, and purchasing the land for right-of-way.

Only a month previously the railroad had trouble finishing its last mile of roadbed from the Jurupa turn to the new depot. Pliny Evans claimed that Vine Street was owned by his Riverside Land and Irrigation Company and as Tom Hays was that company's vice-president, elected the previous January, the railroad would have to deal with him. Evans smilingly said, "I think Hays will now have a most excellent opportunity to even things up with the railroad people." But the railroad's chief civil engineer, Harry Omstead, did not seem too concerned. He said that the road would be finished before long.[5]

Suddenly at midnight, Saturday, February 13th, bonfires were lit along the last section of the rail line. Men sprang into action laying track along Vine from Tenth to Seventh streets. The railroad company had quietly settled with property owner, Mrs. Ida Moore, so that the line could be put through. By working fast Saturday night and all day Sunday they finished the construction before Evans and Tom could get an injunction Monday morning backing their company's claim to the ownership of the street. The newspaper reported that the Salt Lake stole a march over the local troublemakers.[6]

3. *Ibid*, Feb. 10, 1904.
4. *Ibid*, Mar. 23, 1904.
5. *Ibid*. Jan. 30, 1904.
6. *Ibid*, Feb. 15, 1904.

Victoria Club

Other unknown troublemakers a week later broke into the office of attorney Wilfred Peck who, working for the railroad, had uncovered much of Tom's crookedness. Little damage was done but a note written on Peck's office typewriter was left for all to see. It read, "You blackened the name of Tom Hays. You and Gibbons and Ross Clark think you are going to get the grand jury to do great things but you won't get ahead of Tom Hays, Joe Noyes and P. T. Evans." Tom had his supporters.[7]

On March 21st the Riverside County Republican Committee announced Hays was not resigning as chairman and that the committee would stand by him. That evening he presided over a lodge meeting but by midnight he was a fugitive hiding from Sheriff Coburn who had a warrant for his arrest. News had leaked out that a large sum of money was missing from the Orange Growers National Bank and a run on that bank forced it to close at noon. The paper announced that the bank directors and stockholders would make good the losses caused by the former cashier and bank wrecker, Tom Hays. Everyone believed the bank's closing was only temporary. Hopefully there were enough assets to protect the 1400 depositors.

The *Los Angeles Times* was more factual, reporting that the surprise audit by National Bank Examiner Wilson showed a deficit of almost $100,000. The paper went on to say that when Hays resigned from the

---

7. *Ibid*, Feb. 18, 1904.

Salt Lake Depot 1904

bank in November and it was discovered that $5,000 was missing, Hays repaid that sum. Later when another shortage of $18,000 was uncovered and Hays was not able to repay it he gave a trust deed to cover the loss. This money had gone into Kern County oil field options and was unavailable as cash.[8]

Where was Tom Hays? At midnight bank cashier M. J. Twogood got Sheriff Coburn out of bed to issue a warrant for Tom's arrest. When Mrs. Coburn answered the door she saw Hays pass the house. He had been watching the sheriff's residence to learn if a warrant would be issued. That was the last anyone saw of Tom for three days.

Sheriff Coburn searched the Rubidoux Club and the Riverside Country Club on West Eighth Street near Brockton where Lo San the Chinese caretaker was in charge. Tom's Glenwood apartment was vacant; his wife and daughter were at their Ocean Park cottage since their return from an eastern trip. Mrs. Hays, when interviewed by the press, refused to believe her husband had done anything wrong. She also said she knew nothing about those nasty rumors of Tom picnicking in the park with other fascinating company. Mrs. Hays who was reported to be a beautiful, gracious woman with a lovely, golden-haired daughter, professed she had no idea where Tom was and did not believe that he had left Riverside. Some gossips, however, claimed he had gone to Mexico.

---

8. *Ibid*, Mar. 22, 1904.

A March 23rd *Press* editorial entitled "Finding Out the Truth" asked, "What do people think now? They are beginning to recognize no man could spend such money on fast women, whiskey, poker, and politics on a $200 monthly salary. There is no doubt the $1,200 to $1,500 he has been spending monthly has been gotten dishonestly. This last exposure will put an end to the brazen attempts of Hays to continue

Tom as cashier, Daniels at the right in Evans Bank Building

to be a factor in a community that he has debauched and disgraced. He has done more than any man who lived in Riverside to debase our county politics and demoralize our moral standards. Hays now stands revealed in his true light."[9]

That evening a friend of Tom's brought word to Judge Noyes that Hays would surrender to the sheriff if the complaints against him were transferred to Noyes' court. This was accepted and Hays gave himself up. He had been hiding in the attic of the Riverside Country Club where he was carefully looked after by his Chinese friend, Lo San. This clubhouse, built in 1899 on West Eighth Street, was a single-story bungalow with a spacious attic. When quizzed by the sheriff Lo San had cheerfully lied to protect Tom.[10]

Soon the fugitive surrendered and was taken before Judge Noyes.

9. *Ibid.*
10. *Ibid,* Mar. 24, 1904.

This judge owed his political position to Hays who had successfully managed his 1900 campaign for the superior court judgeship. On March 24, 1904 Tom was charged with the embezzlement of $5,000 from the bank and was admitted to bail of $10,000. He left to get bail but was stopped by being informed that three other indictments for theft had just been filed for two amounts of $3,000 and one of $5,000. Noyes raised bail to $40,000 and Tom protested that it was excessive. Bank president Gaylor

Pliny Evans as cartooned by Willard Cundiff

Rouse was sent for and the matter discussed.

Rouse said, "Why Hays, you know you took over $90,000 from the bank."

"Was it as much as that?", Tom asked.

Then knowing that he could not raise the $40,000 bail at 11:00 p.m.

Riverside Public Library Collection

The jail, where Tom stayed

he went quietly to jail with Sheriff Coburn.[11]

The next day while Tom in his cell enjoyed a luncheon sent in from the Glenwood Hotel, U.S. Marshal Henry Osborn served him with a federal warrant because the embezzlement involved a national bank. At their January, 1903 meeting the directors of the Orange Growers Bank had voted to change from a state to a national bank, which meant stricter regulations and federal examinations for the institution. Tom, a bank director since January, 1902 may have been uneasy over these new rules. The directors also established a savings department and took the name of the Orange Growers National Bank.[12]

Before long Hays' wife and 12 year old daughter, Wanda, visited him. They found him occupying a jail cell on the second floor in the then vacant women's section. He occasionally had the privilege of using the telephone in the sheriff's nearby office and friends sent him cigars, liquid refreshments, and flowers. After her visit Mrs. Hays, poised and sweet, told reporters that she had known her husband since she was 14 years old and that this was the first time she had ever known unhappiness.

11. *Ibid.*
12. *Ibid,* Jan. 14, 1903.

A *Press* editorial entitled "No occasion for bouquets" proclaimed that "Tom Hays, gambler, rake, and thief is in jail where he belongs but foolish girls are sending him flowers and other friends are keeping him supplied with cigars and champagne. Is there any occasion for these gifts? We think not! Here is a man who has been unfaithful to his family and untrue to his friends. He has looted a bank and brought undue sufferings to depositors and stockholders. We doubt if the bank directors who must make good his embezzlements are sending any bouquets."[13]

While Tom sat in jail he was the main subject of conversation about town. One of the most interesting stories came from John R. Newberry who in 1883 had helped establish in Riverside the short-lived banking firm of Kleinfelter and Newberry. He now was a very successful Los Angeles merchant, and had been an early director of the Orange Growers Bank. Newberry stated that Hays since his earliest association with the bank had been crooked. In 1892 after working six months in the Orange Growers Bank, Hays overdrew by $1,500 his personal bank account and bought real estate. Newberry, then in charge of finance, had made Hays deed this property to the bank.

Later Hays, having almost no personal funds, "borrowed" money from the bank without permission, and went east. Newberry wired him to return the money at once. This he was slow in doing and when he returned, Newberry demanded in front of bank president Daniels that Hays resign as cashier. Tom refused. Then Newberry said that if anyone would buy his bank stock he would get out. Hays turned to Daniels and told him to buy it; Daniels complied. Hays seemed to have some hold over Daniels that Newberry could never understand. He also stated that as Hay's bank associates knew nothing about banking, it was easy for Tom to get away with anything.[14]

After a few days in jail Tom appeared before the Riverside County Grand Jury which had heard other witnesses relating to the case. With rumpled shirt and uncombed hair he appeared nervous and ill-at-ease. This strongly contrasted with his usual appearance. After a brief questioning Tom stated that because his attorneys John S. Chapman and E. A. Meserve of Los Angeles had been unable to reach Riverside in time for the hearing he did not want to enter a plea until they came.

On March 30th in Judge Noyes' Superior Courtroom in the county courthouse, which still occupied the Arlington Hotel at Eighth and Lime streets, Tom pleaded not guilty on all five counts and proclaimed his

13. *Ibid*, Mar. 26, 1904.
14. *Ibid*, Mar. 24, 1904.

innocence before a crowded courtroom. He was represented by Riverside attorneys Eric Gill, Frank Densmore and Miguel Estudillo. Later with bail increased to $50,000, Hays was taken back to jail as he could not raise that amount.

After hearing much testimony by Riverside people the Los Angeles Federal Grand Jury on April 20th indicted Tom on five counts, two for embezzlement and three for falsifying bank records. When arrested in Riverside on the federal charges Tom, after a month and a half in jail, appeared May 6th before Judge Noyes. Riverside District Attorney Lyman Evans read a letter which requested the release of Hays by the state court so that he could be tried in the U.S. District Court in Los Angeles. Judge Noyes after studying the case released him from state charges and turned him over to Sheriff Coburn acting as U.S. Deputy Marshal. Tom, in custody of the sheriff, took the morning train to Los Angeles where he was arraigned in the federal court. After pleading not guilty he was released on a $30,000 bond furnished by the Aetna Indemnity Company and breathing fresh air again, joined his family at their Ocean Park cottage. Because of the crowded federal court calendar his Los Angeles trial, twice postponed, would not take place until April, 1905, a year after his indictment.

The last of June, 1904 former friends reported that they had seen Hays with a Riverside friend, D. J. Hughes, staying at the California Hotel in San Francisco. Having sold his West Riverside quarry for $10,000, Tom was back leading the good life, entertaining friends, and seeing the sights. It was hard to believe that with a felony charge against him he was out on bail.[15]

---

15. *Ibid,* June 27, 1904.

CHAPTER XIII
The Mess that Tom Left Behind

In Riverside things were not so rosy. The Reverend Goff preached a sermon to the shaken Riverside residents, using as his text the Bible quotation "Wherefore let him that thinketh he standeth take heed lest he fall." With no mention of Tom by name the sermon pointed out that when a person climbs too fast, especially by dishonest methods, he is apt to fall sooner or later.

Before Tom was securely in jail, the Riverside County Grand Jury had been investigating other persons involved with him and his nefarious politics. The *Los Angeles Times* in December, 1903, reported that "if Hays ever comes to court there will be a scurrying for the tall grass, not only by prominent Riverside politicians but by some of the plush in the City of the Angels." The paper charged that, no doubt due to his political influence, Hays got a rake-off on many county deals and had a hand in letting every contract for the building of the new courthouse.[1]

In January, 1904 the Riverside County Grand Jury called Tom, all the county supervisors, and others to testify in a $13,000 courthouse bond swindle and other misuses of county funds. On January 12th the jury indicted C. W. Craven, county supervisor from the second district, for

---

1. *Los Angeles Times*, Dec. 6, 1904.

embezzlement. He was charged with "willfully, unlawfully, feloniously and fraudulently converting and appropriating the said sum of $125.25 in lawful money to his own use." On October 13, 1903 he took this money from the Pacific Lumber Company as his cut on lumber delivered for a county repair job on the West Riverside bridge. A warrant for

Rev. Edward F. Goff   *Charles Brouse*

Courtesy R. L. Haglund

Craven's arrest was issued. After posting bond Craven went back to his job as supervisor.

Two weeks later the grand jury struck again. It filed a request for removal of A. T. Kimbell of Perris and John Shaver of San Jacinto from their positions as county supervisors. While no felony charges were placed against them they were charged with wilful misconduct in office. Kimball was accused of receiving funds for using his own horse teams on the county roads and Shaver with furnishing at a profit, hardware from his store.[2] Laws were explicit that county officials may not do this.

Both Kimbell and Shaver filed demurrers which were sustained in February by a Los Angeles judge who ruled that the statute of limitations prevented any action against them.[3] A year after they commited the offenses the judge also sustained Craven's demurrer but recommended that the next grand jury review his case.

---

2. *Riverside Daily Press*, Jan. 23, 1904.
3. *Ibid*, Feb. 4, 1904.

On March 29, 1904 the grand jury made its final report which warmly roasted the entire board of supervisors. The jury reported that "investigation shows in the matter of appointments by the supervisors, Hays had much influence. Anyone doing county business apparently needed to go through Hays. Supervisor Cravens obtained political support for his reelection by agreeing to buy for $20,000 the Chalmers block for the new courthouse." The jury, moreover, found that building inspector J. W. Caroll and Supervisor Cravens had also collected from laborers and that Supervisors Fred Dunbar and Kimball had collected for road work during 1901, 1902, and 1903. No further indictments, however, were returned.

A new grand jury in an action to remove Cravens from office indicted him on the same charge. A week later on April 29th, it added other charges of receiving bonuses on county hospital construction.

After filing a demurrer Cravens suddenly on May 16th resigned from the Riverside County Board of Supervisors, and returned the sum of $155.77 to the county treasury. The case against him was dismissed as the jury sought only to remove him from office.[4] Sometime later Cravens moved from Riverside and a new appointee to the board of supervisors was under consideration. Supervisor Kimbell was also reindicted. After being tried twice with hung juries he was finally declared not guilty at a third trial and freed to return to his work as country supervisor.[5]

When the Orange Growers National Bank was forced to close on March 22, 1904 following the run caused by Tom's embezzlement, many

4. *Ibid*, May 16, 1904.
5. *Ibid*, Oct. 5, 1904.

people were affected. Chief among these were the bank's directors and stockholders who under the then existing bank laws had to make good the $94,000 loss.

In November, 1903 due to Hays' energetic campaign work, M. J. Daniels had been elected U.S. congressman. Since Daniels spent much time in Washington, D.C., Gaylor Rouse acted as bank president during that period and in January, 1904 became president. He presided over a board of directors composed of Daniels, E. B. Howe, J. C. Hardman, A. A. Caldwell, J. E. Brown, J. G. Baird, C. L. McFarland and H. E. Huntington. M. J. Twogood was cashier and Clyde Daniels assistant cashier.[6]

Following Tom's indictment the bank directors took over most of his remaining Riverside property. Previously the Salt Lake Railroad had attached his 30-acre orange grove on Colton Avenue and a 12-acre grove in Arlington Heights to cover its $12,000 loss. Hays had already deeded to his wife three lots in the Orange Growers Bank's addition. The bank acquired his newly finished Mt. Rubidoux bungalow which it later sold to the Pattee and Lett families. The bank also attached Tom's quarter interest in the Rubidoux Heights real estate development. On May 20th he and his wife Bertha deeded all rights and interest in this property to Robert L. Bettner for $3,000 which Bettner paid to the bank's receiver.[7] It was believed that Tom's funds were running low and that he was mortgaging his Ocean Park cottage.

Many of the stockholders who lost heavily in the bank's failure were relatives and old acquaintances of M. J. Daniels. An old Minnesota friend, William Waite, came to Riverside with his family in 1898 to retire. He bought a house on Brockton Avenue and a five acre orange grove. The rest of his savings went into Orange Growers Bank stock making him the bank's third largest stockholder. The day the bank closed he, like many others, went to the courthouse and put his home and grove in his wife's name. These were all he managed to save of his life's earnings and as a consequence spent his old age in regret and poor financial circumstancs.[8]

Daniels' nephew, Captain R. W. Ozmun of Tustin, was the bank's largest stockholder. He had inherited much wealth from his father who was president of the Columbia Savings Bank of Los Angeles and possessed stock in other banks. Young Ozmun was considered Orange County's wealthiest citizen, owning a great deal of land as well as bank stock. Soon after the failure of the Orange Growers National Bank he suffered

6. *Ibid*, Mar. 23, 1904.
7. Riverside County Courthouse Deeds, Book 168, p. 306.
8. Interview with Dr. Elizabeth Harper, 1969, (granddaughter).

a nervous breakdown. One year later on April 30, 1905 he died of a stroke at the age of 29, leaving a wife and two small sons. This was two days after Tom's Los Angeles trial ended.[9]

Gaylor Rouse not only lost his personal investment but his mercantile store, called Rouse's, was severely affected and its capital tied up. For a while it looked as if the store would close but some temporary loans saved it until later when its funds were released. Also due to these difficulties the marriage of his son Charles to Estelle McIntosh, a graduate nurse living in Colton, was delayed a month.[10] Other Riversiders experienced similar troubles and there was general apprehension over the situation.

Aided by bank officers G. Rouse, M. J. Twogood, C. Daniels, and Charles Brouse, Bank Examiner J. W. Wilson went to work on the books of the bank. It was rumored that the new Citizens Bank would absorb the closed institution.

The Citizens Bank first opened for business July 3, 1903 in the Reynolds Hotel Block on the southeast corner of Main and Ninth streets.[11] It began modestly as a state bank with $50,000 capital, but grew rapidly and became in a few years Riverside's strongest bank. Its founder and first president, Stephen H. Herrick, was an astute businessman who told friends he decided to organize a new bank for Riverside because he felt too many local bankers were crooked.[12]

Before coming to Riverside in 1885, Herrick served as mayor of Grinnell, Iowa, and as president of the Grinnell Savings Bank. With former Iowa Governor Samuel Merrill and A. J. Twogood of Riverside, he founded the East Riverside Land Company which developed the area now known as Highgrove. Later he was also president of the Riverside Highland Water Company, the Lemona Heights Company, and the Monte Vista Citrus Association.[13]

On May 2, 1904 Bank Receiver Wilson announced that the Citizens Bank would absorb the defunct Orange Growers National Bank as soon as audits of both banks were completed. Two weeks later Wilson said that he had found the Citizens Bank in excellent condition and the consolidation could take place. On May 13th the Citizens Bank moved into the Evans Building which was formerly occupied by Tom and his bank. With this bank merger the Orange Growers National Bank ceased to exist, but its old depositors now had accounts with the Citizens Bank and were free to withdraw their funds. Few did so as they had strong confidence in president Herrick and bank directors C. H. Low, C. Van

---

9. *Los Angeles Times*, May 1, 1905.
10. Interview with Mrs. Charles Rouse, 1966.
11. *Riverside Daily Press*, July 3, 1903.
12. Information Joan Herrick Hall, 1971.
13. *Ibid.*

Zwalenburg, D. W. McLeod, G. H. Dole, J. A. Allen, P. D. Cover, J. F. Humphreys, B. Stephenson, D. P. Chapman, and H. W. Leighton. W. B. Clancy, former county auditor, was cashier and Carl Derby, assistant cashier.

S. H. Herrick
Riverside Public Library Collection

On July 16, 1904 the Citizens Bank issued its first annual statement showing deposits of over half a million dollars and total resources of $682,215. It had borrowed $75,000 to absorb the defunct bank but this was quickly repaid. The $180,000 owed by the Orange Growers Bank had been paid and its $320,000 in deposits were again available to the depositors. A slow, painful three year liquidation with receivership and its harmful consequences to the community had been avoided.[14] In

14. *Riverside Daily Press*, July 16, 1904.

October the Citizens Bank opened a branch in nearby Arlington, doubled its capital to $100,000, and became a national bank. Its outstanding service to the community was rewarded by increased patronage.

MAGNOLIA AVENUE, RIVERSIDE, CAL.

The Greatest Orange Growing County IN THE WORLD.

Politics also took a turn for the better with Tom no longer in Riverside. On May 10th the Riverside County Republican Convention, presided over by Chairman C. O. Baker, met at the Loring Opera House. While proceedings may not have been as colorful as previously, delegates accomplished a good deal. Miguel Estudillo, a Riverside lawyer who had long fought the Hays faction in politics, was nominated for state assemblyman. M. J. Daniels received a nominal but unenthusiastic endorsement for reelection. By June, however, he was out of the race and his political career was finished. The convention also endorsed E. W. Holmes for county supervisor as a replacement for Cravens. Holmes, editor of the *Riverside Daily Press* had exposed many of the corrupt acts of that board during the last two years. The *Los Angeles Times* rejoiced in what it called a strong defeat for the "Hays gang."[15]

Previously the *Times* had been very critical not only of Tom but of W. W. Phelps, C. W. Craven, P. T. Evans, District Attorney Lyman Evans, the *Enterprise*, and especially Superior Court Judge Noyes. In an editorial dated March 28, 1904, the *Times* printed, ". . . the attitude of

15. *Los Angeles Times*, May 11, 1904.

J. Noyes of the Superior Court proceedings involving an effort to permit the unlimited exposure of Hays' crookedness and the grand jury fiasco which resulted in the dropping of the Hays' case so far as it appertained to the Salt Lake Railroad matter have stained the official ermine of Judge Noyes so indelibly that he can never hope to live down in this state the disgrace he has brought upon himself . . . . What of that gang of leeches who so feasted and waxed fat upon the patronage and support of the master rascal Tom Hays? What of these coyotes who when the leader of the band raised his voice in denial and protest lifted their noses toward the moon and made a wild chorus and yelped themselves hoarse in his behalf." Judge Noyes a week later filed a $100,000 libel suit against the *Times* for defamation of character which he later dropped.

Riverside County Clerk W. W. Phelps also filed a libel suit against the *Times* and in July won a $12,000 judgment against it and Harrison Gray Otis, owner. The *Riverside Daily Press* rejoiced in the decision saying the *Times* should quit its malicious and slandering abuse of all who incurred its displeasure. It also pointed out that not all Riversiders were crooked horse thieves and that it might be expensive to use such terms.[16] General Otis was reported to be upset and possibly fearful as six weeks later the *Times* apologized to Lyman Evans. Saying that as its March 23rd article, which seriously reflected on Evans' integrity, was found to be untrue it withdrew its unwarranted charge.[17] The *Times*, however, appealed the Phelps decision and on December 25, 1904 in Judge Hughes' Los Angeles court a compromise was worked out. Phelps received only $2,500 from the *Times* and due to the expense decided not to continue his fight. The *Press*, deploring the punitive amount, declared it was a moral victory and probably was the only libel suit the *Times* had not appealed to the Supreme Court.[18]

Slowly politics and city life returned to normal and newspaper headlines dealt mostly with the Russo-Japanese War and the completion of the new Riverside County Courthouse. By the last of May, 1904 most of the details of the building were finished. However, in reply to questioning by a grand jury committee, building inspector Carroll said that the roof was unsatisfactory as the surface did not meet specifications and pools of rain water could not run off. After considerable difficulty and expense a new roof was installed under the architect's supervision. The sub-contractor had done a cheap job, not bothering to properly mop in the composition paper with asphalt.[19]

On June 23rd the supervisors accepted the completed courthouse,

16. *Riverside Daily Press*, July 25, 1904.
17. *Ibid*, Sept. 17, 1904.
18. *Ibid*, Dec. 24, 1904.
19. *Minutes*, Riverside County Board of Supervisors.

Riverside Municipal Museum Collection   *Corridor, Riverside County Court House*

subject to the finishing of some painting. The building had cost $137,750 but extras had raised the total expense to $159,422. Of this $119,566 had been paid, leaving a balance of $39,856 due. A week later the county officers and employees began moving into the new building, leaving the Arlington Hotel which for ten years had housed the county courts and offices.

When opened to the public the new courthouse was impressive. Its rows of stately Ionic columns, figure sculpture, monumental granite steps, and decorative cast iron and globe lights, all reflected the popular style of Beaux-Art Classicism. On the four front corners of the building a dozen pressed-zinc sculptured maidens of noble and resolute bearing reposed in groups of three. Upon arriving from Chicago they were installed by E. L. Quinn who said that hopefully they would look like stone when painted the same color as the courthouse. Each group consisted of two seated maidens and Justice who stood helmeted and well draped, holding a sword or spear in one hand and her scale balance in the other. In Riverside she is not blind but for some reason was installed without her wings. The newspaper remarked that, "maybe these wings are omitted as a compromise with the knockers who insist Justice never had wings anyhow."[20] The wings, shown in the architectural drawings, may have been difficult to attach.

20. *Riverside Daily Press*, April 25, 1904.

Riverside County Courthouse

Riverside Municipal Museum Collection

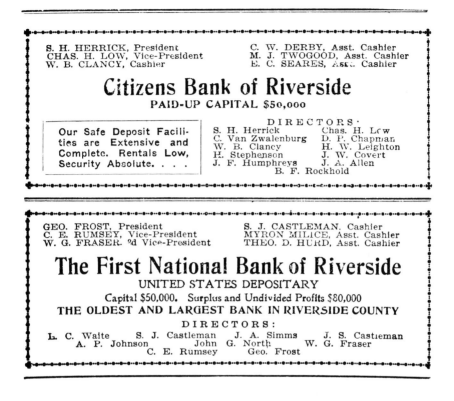
Inside, the high, arched ceiling, pillars, dome, and pilastered walls
of the main corridor shone brilliantly white. Soft light entered from
the pale colored glass windows. The wainscoting of white tile and light
brown marble contrasted with the dark woodwork. While over the large
central doorway leading into the Superior Courtroom a sculptured Justice
surrounded by representative persons looked down on the ever-passing
flow of people seeking her favors. Only the coarsely finished cement
floor seemed out of place with the other elegant details. Walls of the
courthouse rooms painted a soft white often had quarter-sawed oak
wainscoting. Carpets or linoleum of brown and dull green harmonized
with the new heavy oak and leather furniture. The substantial quality
of the building was appreciated by everyone and the supervisors thanked
the architects and the contractor for a generally fine job.[21]

On July 5th the board of supervisors, then consisting of F. M.

---

21. *Riverside Daily Press*, June 30, 1904.

Dunbar, chairman, A. T. Kimbell, J. Shaver, J. T. Hamner, and newly appointed E. W. Holmes met for the first time in their new east room. They approved the purchase of the oak and leather furniture from the George H. Fuller Desk Company and the golden oak and metal desks and tables from the Yawman-Erble Company of San Francisco. The latter furniture was considered very elegant, being made of japanned and pickled steel and trimmed with mouldings, grills and brackets of pure bronze.[22]

They closed that first meeting by reducing the salary of Dr. C. Van Zwalenburg, county health officer, to $25 a month. In a letter to the board the doctor said he would resign if this were done. When Holmes asked why the old board members had failed to consult with the doctor before taking this action, he was ignored. While county citizens thus may have questioned the quality of some of their supervisors everyone seemed pleased with Riverside's new attractive courthouse.

22. *Minutes*, Riverside County Board of Supervisors.

Los Angeles

CHAPTER XIV

The Trial of the Bank Wrecker

From May, 1904 while Tom Hays was out on bond, he had lived quietly in Ocean Park with his family. He worked a little in Los Angeles real estate and looked after the few pieces of property he and his wife still owned. He maintained an office with his bonding company which saved him from visiting them often;[1] also he still had an important interest in the Aetna Oil Company which had much property in the Bakersfield area. One thing was certain, he avoided Riverside where there were still many unpleasant reminders of his former activities. Only once did he return when on the night of August 5th he made a fast motor car run accompanied by Sheriff Coburn. They got Judge Stephenson out of bed to approve Tom's bond and thus keep him out of jail. Hays, at the instigation of Los Angeles District Attorney Valentine, had been rearrested on the old Riverside charges. Tom moved so fast that night that neither his old friends nor his enemies caught a glimpse of him.

On March 29, 1905 Hays went to trial in Los Angeles before Superior Judge Olin Wellborn. This judge was noted for his honesty and fairness. For almost a month the defendant sat in the United States Circuit Court which occupied the fourth floor of the Tajo Building at the corner of First and Broadway. He was to be tried on the six counts named by

---

1. *Riverside Daily Press*, Nov. 18, 1904.

the Federal Grand Jury when it indicted him in May, 1904. These were two counts for embezzling funds of $5,000 and $1,000 from the Orange Growers National Bank, one for making a false report to the comptroller of the currency concerning the condition of the bank, and three counts for false entries in the bank's books.

A few days before the trial United States District Attorney L. H. Valentine, who was in charge of the prosecution, announced, "It's states prison for Hays. He is being tried on a felony charge and the statutes are very clear that if convicted he must be sent there."[2] When the trial opened Hays and his three defense lawyers sat at a table on one side of the courtroom. These attorneys were John S. Chapman, E. A. Meserve and Earl Rogers, all of Los Angeles.[3]

Chapman, then considered the dean of the Los Angeles Bar, had had a long and successful career dealing with land and water litigation. He had known Tom for some years as he had participated in lawsuits between the oil scrippers and mineral claimants which had also involved Tom's Aetna Oil Company. Chapman's stocky body was usually encased in a long, loose coat. He had a dome-shaped head and a serious face framed by grey hair and a short beard. His presence and speech radiated dignity and authority.

Earl Rogers, in contrast to Chapman, was only 36 years of age and known as the best criminal lawyer in the district. He was impeccably dressed, tall, thin, and restless. He had dark hair parted in the middle and piercing blue eyes that could see right through a witness. Rogers' father, the Reverend Lowell Rogers, had been Tom's high school teacher in Lancaster, Pennsylvania. The families had been friends for over twenty years and Hays was affectionately called "Uncle Tom" by various members of Rogers' family.[4]

The third defense lawyer, E. A. Meserve, was known as an excellent corporation attorney. He gave the impression of being a plump, cheerful man as he looked over his glasses in a rather amused way as though he had a card up his sleeve. These men were indeed a rather remarkable trio.

At a similar table on the opposite side of the room sat the United States prosecuting attorneys, L. H. Valentine and his deputy, George L. McKeeby, who were both able men but less colorful than the defending attorneys. These lawyers spent the first day and a half of the trial examining prospective jurors until 12 men were selected.

The next day a *Los Angeles Times* headline read, "Hays Smiles in Torture. The Trial of Bank Wrecker Finally Begins." The first witness

---

2. *Los Angeles Times*, Mar. 27, 1905.
3. *Ibid*, April 1, 1905. Also Case 1918, Federal Record Center, Bell, Calif.
4. *Riverside Daily Press*, Jan. 12, 1907.
   and Adela St. Johns, *Final Verdict*, (New York, 1962).

was the ruined bank's former president M.-J. Daniels who was also father-in-law of cashier M. J. Twogood. Under questioning Daniels said he was away from the bank much of the time and was ignorant of Tom's embezzlements.

Chapman cross-examined, "When were you elected to Congress?"

"In the fall of 1902."

"Did Hays take an active part in your campaign?"

"I—I think he did."

"Wasn't he absent from Riverside much of the time?"

"I—I couldn't say. Well, he was chairman of the Riverside Central Committee so had to go to Sacramento."

"How much time did Hays give to your campaign?"

"Well, I don't know. I can't say what time. He done a reasonable amount of work; there wasn't a good deal of correspondence. He went to Santa Barbary (sic) and done what he could in my behalf. I will say he done very good work for me."

"Did you check to see if the bank could afford the last declared five percent dividend? Was this action recorded?"

"No—o, Hays said we could afford the dividend. He said he kept all information on slips and did not have time to record them. Hays was so busy." The next day the paper announced, "Daniels He Did Wiggle."[5]

Gaylor Rouse was next to testify when the trial resumed on April 4th. He said that Hays had not kept any bank minutes from March 28, 1902 to July, 1903. In January, 1903 the Orange Growers Bank changed from a state to a national bank and the law then required the cashier to keep the minutes and records up-to-date and the bank president to sign them. This had not been done and the bank directors were ignorant of this neglect. Now the bank's *Minutes Book* could not be found.

On the following day Tom appeared crushed, and the life drained out of him; he had lost his confident swagger and was pale and disheveled. He had just received word that Mr. Steigwait, his wife's father, an old Pennsylvania Dutchman, had died. He had left $25,000 in insurance and several thousands more in property to Tom and his wife. Steigwait had always adored his son-in-law and never doubted his honesty.[6]

Earl Rogers rose and asked for one day's continuance saying that the district attorney had consented. The judge set the following day for the trial's resumption. When it resumed the lawyers for the defense suggested it was not Hays but the bank directors who were responsible for the missing bank minutes. Rouse admitted that Riverside County

5. *Los Angeles Times*, April 1, 1905.
6. *Ibid*, April 5, 1905.

Treaurer Mitchell had suggested that the bank go on Hays' bond with a security company and as a favor Mitchell would deposit county funds with the bank. This was carried out as agreed.

"This," said attorney Chapman in a ringing voice, "might explain why some of the bank's minutes were not written up and why the directors do not want them produced."

It began to appear that if Hays had to go to jail he might take other bank officers with him. By Thursday Hays' lawyers were in a

Louis H. Valentine

bitter fight with attorney Valentine who wanted the bank's books produced, for without them the conviction of Hays would be almost impossible. The defense lawyers, questioning M. J. Twogood, tried to show that the books were totally inaccurate and that there was no need to produce them.[7]

Later testimony revealed, according to the newspapers, the "Methods of Bank Thief. How His Institution was Brazenly Robbed; The True State of Affairs. The brass bound, copper-riveted nerve with which Hays robbed the bank made the spectators gape with astonishment."

M. J. Twogood testified how Hays would take the total of checks

7. *Ibid*, April 7 ,1905.

cashed for a day, tack on four or five thousand dollars and enter the increased sum in the general ledger. He would cut down the day's deposits by an equal amount and enter the wrong total in the ledger. If anyone had taken the trouble to compare the ticket book with the general ledger Hays would have been caught but no one ever bothered to check.

In March, 1904 the first evidence of Tom's embezzlements was uncovered when Clyde Daniels, bookeeper and son of the bank's president, called Twogood's attention to some of these discrepancies. Then the two men went over the books. Whenever Twogood was away due to his wife's illness, these discrepancies would appear. For instance, on September 6, 1901 the adding ticket slip showed the total of checks cashed was $11,380, while entry in the general ledger was $14,380. This gave Hays a nice $3,000 profit. Twogood identified the handwriting as Hays'.[8] During this testimony Hays was very busy with his papers. He appeared disturbed and avoided looking at people. At the end of the day he left at once, dashing down the three flights of stairs to avoid the crowded elevator.

The next day was a bad one for the prosecution. Earl Rogers made a ridiculous spectacle of the Orange Growers National Bank when the bank's individual ledger was brought out. He defied the district attorneys to find a single correct total in it. Defense attorney Meserve demanded that an adding machine be brought into court so that Clyde Daniels and Twogood could make a test. The totals were full of errors. The following day dragged with Daniels on the stand most of the day. A summary of his testimony revealed that the year's total deposit slips showed $502,508 while the ledger recorded $407,547. Where had the $94,960 gone? The paper suggested that only the bland smiling Howard Thomas Hays could answer that question. Then Daniels revealed how totally Hays had been in charge of the bank. During some of these bookkeeping details a few jurors dozed.[9]

Later two young Riverside bank clerks, Charles Brouse and E. M. Hillegas, gave Hays a bad time. Brouse told how he "unwittingly helped Hays fake the report to the controller," how Hays had worked all night in the bank trying totals, until he finally found one that would balance and could stand examination the next morning. Bank commissioner J. R. Wilson had arrived unexpectedly. Brouse said he did not realize until later what was going on. He also testified to the famous $94,000 shortage found when Hays was not there. This was the most damaging evidence so far against Hays. Hillegas repeated Brouse's testimony and then added

8. *Ibid*, April 11, 1905.
9. *Los Angeles Times*, April 12, 1905.

that he and Brouse had read the testimonial sheets in District Attorney Valentine's office while waiting to testify. Defense lawyers grinned!

Attorney Meserve gravely rose to his feet and addressed the judge, "The order of this court excluding witnesses from this trial has been violated in spirit and fact. I request all the testimony of Brouse and Hillegas be stricken out." After considerable argument the judge concurred. Earl Rogers danced up and down. He had an injured hand

J. S. Chapman

bandaged like a boxing glove which he waved in the air as he questioned Brouse and Hillegas. The two did not realize that what they had done was illegal. All their important testimony against Hays was stricken from the record.[10]

A few days later Dr. E. B. Howe, vice-president of the bank, told how Tom had shed salty tears when he was told by the directors he would have to resign when the Salt Lake Railroad fraud was revealed. Hays said that was no way to treat an important bank cashier and he would not resign without a resolution from the bank commending his honesty

---

10. *Ibid*, April 14, 1905.

and character. The bank weakly gave it to him. The prosecuting attorney after further questioning about the bank's affairs remarked it was a wonder, considering everything, that Hays had not stolen the safe's doors.[11]

The following day the bookkeeping details were dropped and young Riverside Justice of the Peace Thomas B. Stephenson testified, "On the night of March 21, 1904 I was awakened at 11 p.m. and told to issue a complaint and warrant for the arrest of Hays. Later he was brought to my court under arrest and admitted to bail. The complaint was for $1,000 embezzlement on the Hutchison and Brown account." Earl Rogers was quite gay with the young witness, interrupting him by asking him if he wasn't rather young for such a responsible job.[12] On April 19 Lo San, steward of the Riverside Country Club where Hays had hidden, perjured himself before the court to favor Hays. The Chinaman was arrested but Tom furnished bond and got Earl Rogers to defend him successfully.

The trial dragged on with some unimportant witnesses testifying until on April 26th Earl Rogers gave one of the most brilliant arguments ever made at a court trial in Los Angeles. The speech was brief, to the point, and it crackled. He practically accused M. J. Daniels and cashier Twogood of prosecuting Hays to hide their own guilt. He cleverly clouded the main trial issues by directing attacks at the amazing methods with which the Orange Growers National Bank had carried on its business.

Rogers next severely criticized Judge Noyes. "What shall we think when a Superior Judge of Riverside has to compare his testimony six times with someone else before he can go on the witness stand? Maybe it is because Hays is no longer chairman of the County Central Republican Committee." Rogers pointed out there was an unexplained $30,000 bank shortage with which Hays was not involved. He said Hays hid because he was reluctant to go before a magistrate at night when he knew he could not get bail. Hays was described by Rogers as a misunderstood victim of dishonest men whose banking methods were confused and illegal. It was apparent Rogers' eloquent and emotional appeal had touched the jury.

The next day attorney Valentine presented the case for the prosecution before a crowd of people gathered to hear the end of the trial. It was noted that there were at least a dozen women also present in the packed courtroom. Valentine's final arguments were cool, dispassionate, and unemotional. He defended the Daniels family while pointing out instance after instance of Tom's dishonesty and thefts, saying there was

11. *Los Angeles Times*, April 15, 1905.
12. Criminal Case, 1918, U.S. Federal Record Center, Bell, Calif.

no doubt of his guilt. Defense attorney Meserve repeated the main theme that others were guilty but his speech failed to have the same emotional impact as Rogers'.[13]

The final arguments of the other prosecuting attorney McKeeby were of interest because for years he had been a strong personal friend of Hays. Now he argued intelligently for Hay's conviction. Suddenly one of the jurors, an old man with an ashen white face, tottered out of

Earl Rogers

the jury box, staggered past the judge and disappeared through the courtroom door. Various men rushed after him and succeeded in catching him as he fell unconscious in the hall. He was John McArthur, a wealthy retired man from Ocean Park, who had recently suffered with intestinal difficulties. A silence hung over the courtroom, everyone feared that perhaps the trial would have to be repeated. Finally a doctor was found who revived the sick man. After a brief consultation, the doctor advised the judge that the juror would be able to return to jury

13. *Los Angeles Times*, April 21, 1905.

duty after the weekend. The judge then dismissed the court to recon-
vene the following Monday.

On that day with all jurors present, Judge Wellborn read the law

to the jury. He offered no advice, preferring to let the jury members
make their own decisions. In the quiet courtroom while the judge was
instructing the jury a little "trial man" shot into the courtroom and
wiggled through the crowd to his usual seat in the front row. He was
bent, poorly clad, and out of breath. For the last 15 years this little old
man had been a spectator at nearly all the big Los Angeles trials. At one
time he had been a good workman but now was poor because he could
not bear to miss the fascinating trials of the criminal courts. He had
missed much of the Hays trial because two other important cases were
being tried simultaneously.

At 3:30 P.M., April 27, after 29 days of testimony, the case went
to the jury. Two hours later the panel returned for further instructions
from Judge Wellborn and then withdrew to deliberate 24 more hours.
The courtroom began to empty, various attorneys went to their offices,
and Earl Rogers left the city to visit another client. Tom was now alone
with Meserve in his office to wait out the tedious hours. The long trial
had been a strain and the agonizing wait began to show. Tom was white-
faced with dark shadows of weariness under his eyes. In his dishevelled
clothes he paced the office. Finally word came that the jury had reached
a decision. The judge returned to receive the verdict, "NOT GUILTY!"

Judge Wellborn acted dazed and seemed to take no heed of the
commotion caused by friends congratulating Tom. Finally the judge

rapped for order, polled the jurors, certified the verdict, and coldly dismissed them. The jury foreman as he stepped down turned fiery red to the roots of his hair. Other jury members acted embarrassed as they left the room. Newspaper men who asked the judge for a statement saw him throw up his hands as he said, "Don't ask me. It is impossible at this time to say anything." He was walking up and down and those who knew him best said they never saw him so upset.

Prosecuting attorney Valentine could only mutter, "I am what you might call thunderstruck."[14]

Tom and his defense attorneys were jubilant. They, with some of Tom's friends, left the courtroom and finding the elevator too slow took the marble steps down two at a time. In Meserve's office Tom was almost incoherent, finally saying, "This is a—a—a—righteous verdict. I believed in it and it came true. What more can I say?"[14]

---

14. *Ibid*, April 29, 1905.

Street Palms

CHAPTER XV

Riverside Revolted
Turns To Civic Beauty

Tom Hays was free. People in Riverside were stunned and many felt Tom had bribed the jury. This may have been a possibility, for on April 30th the *Times* reported that the Federal Secret Service men were looking into bribery charges against some jury members. Nothing, however, came of this investigation.

One pertinent fact discussed by the local newspaper was that Mr. Neuner, the jury foreman, was an old time friend of Tom's and for years had done business with him. This was not revealed until after the trial was finished.[1]

On the first ballot the jury voted 9 to 3 for acquittal and then Neuner went after the three holdouts to free Tom. Two of the three changed their vote but old Mr. McArthur refused, saying that he knew Tom was a crook. So the rest of the jury decided not to go to bed until they reached a verdict. Finally McArthur, tired and sick, gave up. When the leaden-eyed jury, weary from loss of sleep and heated discussions, filed into their box and announced their not guilty verdict it was noted that Judge

---

1. *Riverside Daily Press*, April 29, 1905.

Wellborn omitted his usual thanks for a job well done.

Although the trial had been conducted with courtesy and good nature it proved costly. The total, estimated at $30,000, made it the most expensive case to that date ever tried in the Los Angeles U.S. District Court. Witness costs were $1,500; jurors fees, $684; and stenography expense, $1,150. Rumors were that Tom had paid his three lawyers $5,000 each. In view of the fact that Tom's yearly salary was only $2,400 when he had to leave the bank, these costs seemed exorbitant.[2]

Comments by neighboring newspapers varied from, "Hays escaped because he had the money to pay," to "Seldom have the defects of the jury system been more forcibly portrayed than in the trial of H. T. Hays." Even as far away as Sacramento editors wrote, "This miscarriage of justice has aroused deep and universal indignation in the southern counties."

The local *Press* announced "Justice is not only blind but perverse and perverted as well." Riversiders found the news hard to believe and felt some graft was responsible for the failure to convict. On the other hand, if Tom had been found guilty there probably would have been much sympathy for him.

On May 30th, only two days after the trial's end, Reverend Goff preached a sermon to his Congregational parishioners on the moral lessons of the acquittal of "Bank Wrecker Hays." The Reverend stated, "A grave blow has been struck at public morality. The defendant lawyers are said to be overjoyed by their victory but after being engaged in such a contest and cruelly besmirching the reputation of honorable men, it would be more to their credit if they were represented as going home and taking a bath . . . .

"There are some salutary results from this deplorable case. Henceforth in Riverside no man of that type will be able to secure and hold a position of public trust. The day for such men is past. It will behoove bankers and all who handle the money of others to walk circumspectly. From this day forward the people will require a higher standard of character in those who aspire to political influence and leadership . . . Hays may have escaped our courts but he has not eluded the operation of that higher law. To be ostracized; to have lost forever the friendship, confidence, and respect of the good; to be looked upon as the corrupter of youth, the betrayer of trusts, what more awful harvest could one reap? This man has forgotten the noble ideals of his early years, lived a swinish life of pleasure, called evil good and good evil . . . . We pity him. 'Be not

2. *Ibid*, April 27, 1905.

Pier Ave., Ocean Park, Cal.

deceived; God is not mocked: for whatsoever a man soweth, that shall he also reap!' "

After the trial Tom rejoined his family in Ocean Park. There he could be seen almost every afternoon strolling along Pier Avenue jauntily taking the sea breezes. This was reported by vacationing Riversiders who carefully avoided him while at that ocean resort.[3]

In Riverside there was uncertainty what to do about further prosecution of the Hays case. As all ten indictments against him in the state courts were quashed before the beginning of the federal trial, there remained only the possibility of some action against him in the Riverside Superior Court on three embezzlement charges. The former directors of the Orange Growers National Bank and District Attorney Lyman Evans consulted. Those who had lost heavily wanted the matter pushed. People, however, in a position to act hesitated because of the cost and their lack of confidence in the evidence which had failed to convict in the Los Angeles trial. Also the statute of limitations would soon make further action impossible. The *Times* reported that Riverside, thoroughly sick of the Hays case, appeared in the mood to do nothing.[4]

Riversiders, as though hoping to renew their civic pride, turned with zeal to tree planting, park improvements, and construction. Horse racing,

3. *Ibid*, May 25, 1905.
4. *Los Angeles Times*, June 2, 1905.

polo, tennis, rollerskating, and ocean bathing at Oceanside, Laguna or Newport Beach also furnished pleasure and diversion. Under the leadership of John H. Reed, city tree warden, the Chamber of Commerce undertook to raise funds for a tree planting program to beautify the streets. Except for the planting of pepper trees by the early colonists, the city prior to 1904 had had no general plan.

In April, 1905 an enthusiastic crowd met in the Loring Opera House and heard C. M. Loring, Cornelius Rumsey, and Frank Miller speak on civic beauty and tree planting. That year over a thousand trees were planted; in 1906 twelve hundred were added; and in 1907 fifteen hundred more; all were purchased with funds donated to the Chamber of Commerce. Many palm and pepper trees were added to the bare streets in the northwest section of the mile square. C. M. Loring, who owned property on West Sixth Street, planted at his own expense a mile of peppers and palms on Brockton Avenue south of First Street. The feathery topped pepper tree with its gnarled trunk was the most favored for its shade, easy care, and drought resistance.[5]

Captain C. M. Dexter, now city park superintendent, also collected money for trees. He wanted more planted in Fairmount Park. The city after receiving a gift of land and water from S. C. Evans, built in November, 1903 a dam which formed a seven acre lake in the park.[6] Row boats could be rented for a small fee but rowers claimed that the lake was too shallow and the oars stuck in the mud. Dancing was enjoyed at the park pavilion which in 1902 had been built with $500 in donated funds collected by Dexter and $500 more suplied by the city. Earlier many memorial trees had been planted in the park and watered from a well dug there. The grass of the large picnic areas was cut with a machine pulled by Rex, Riverside's first fire horse. In July, 1905 Rex, then 21 years old, was retired to a life of ease and beauty in Fairmount Park.[7]

During this period the road into Fairmount was improved, enabling automobiles for the first time to come directly to the park. This added greatly to its popularity. Dexter, planning further improvements, collected donations for building a 40 by 150 foot swimming pool. By September, 1905 he had $1,200 but needed $800 more to begin construction. This swimming pool, however, was not constructed until 1912.[8] Contractor Paul H. Ehlers completed it in February at a cost of $3,970. A few months later he built a connecting pumphouse, dressing rooms, a large wading pool for children and connecting sidewalks. The pools were

5. *Riverside Daily Press*, Aug. 8, 1904.
6. *Ibid*, Nov. 21, 1903.
7. *Ibid*, July 18, 1905.
8. *Minutes*, Riverside City Council, Feb. 13, 1912.

The swimming pool at Fairmount

first opened in June and by that time an attractive boat house was also finished.

All during his life Frank Miller was concerned with park development and tree planting. Throughout this period he kept adding to his hotel. In August, 1903 just six months after he finished the main building, he extended the dining room to the west. Three large brick arches connected the new 50 by 60 foot area to the original building. This additional space enabled him to serve the large groups which often came on winter tours.

His new hotel, proving very popular and profitable, required hiring and housing more employees. In July, 1905 Miller started construction of a $30,000 building on Sixth Street just north of the hotel. The red tile brick structure would have rooms for his women employees on the second and third floors, a big steam laundry on the main floor, and a 300 horsepower electric plant in the basement. Additions would later be made to this building.[9]

In the fall of 1905 the city erected a new mission-designed firehouse on Eighth Street near Lime.[10] It had a fire bell on the roof and housed a big engine purchased the previous year. This engine was

9. *Riverside Daily Press,* July 27, 1905.
10. *Ibid,* July 25, 1905.

pulled by two heavy dray horses, called Cap and Mac, which had cost the city $450 for the pair. This firehouse and equipment was under the care of Firechief Joseph Schneider and his "fire laddies."[11]

Other buildings of great service to the city were the hospitals. On December 5, 1901 at the home of Dr. C. Van Zwalenburg a group of local doctors met to organize a hospital to serve the city. In January, 1900 Dr. Van Zwalenburg had come to Riverside from Kalamazoo, Michigan, with his wife and three daughters. There he had practiced for

Eighth Street Firehouse

ten years following his graduation from the University of Michigan. While establishing a medical practice in Riverside he felt keenly the lack of hospital facilities. Assisted by Dr. C. G. Gill and other doctors he succeeded in raising $25,000 through the sale of hospital stock to the doctors and the public.[12] On August 1, 1902 all subscribers to this stock held a meeting to form the corporation. The physicians agreed to act in an advisory capacity and subscribe at least one hundred dollars each but they requested that businessmen manage the association. Directors elected at that meeting were George Frost, president, and George Reynolds, George Bittinger, Lyman Evans and A. N. Younglove.[13] The association leased an old 12-room house on the southwest corner of

11. *Ibid*, Dec. 7, 1904.
12. *Ibid*, Dec. 6, 1901.
13. *Ibid*, Aug. 5, 1902.

Riverside Hospital

Orange and Eleventh streets. After furnishing the rooms the hospital opened on October 30, 1902 for its first surgical operation. It supplied many badly needed facilities but soon proved inadequate.

By 1903 the same group of doctors who had worked hard for the first hospital now undertook a new drive for funds to build larger facilities. In May, 1904 a new Riverside Hospital was completed on Brockton Avenue between Eleventh and Twelfth streets. On the first floor were the administration offices and nine patient rooms and on the second floor were eight single rooms and two large wards. When the city accepted this building, it became Riverside's first community owned hospital, managed by the Riverside Hospital Association. On May 21, 1904 Miss Caldwell, the superintendent, moved her nurses and their patients into the new hospital. It proved very successful and before long was self supporting.[14]

During this period of city development the Salt Lake Railroad's lawsuit against Tom for the return of $8,000 of misappropriated funds was still pending. The railroad claimed he had acquired these funds illegally between January, 1902 and October, 1903 when he acted as its right-of-way agent.

After two postponements the trial without jury began February 13, 1906 in Los Angeles before Judge Olin Wellborn who had presided during the first court case. Defense attorneys were Earl Rogers and E. A. Meserve who had helped Tom before. But J. S. Chapman was

---

14. *Ibid*, May 26, 1904.

too busy with a water suit in San Bernardino to assist this time. Attorneys Oscar Lawler and A. S. Halsted, acting for the railroad, subpoenaed a long list of Riverside property owners and real estate agents. The court ordered cashier C. L. McFarland of the Citizens Bank which had absorbed the defunct bank to produce all canceled checks and records pertinent to the case. Defense lawyers and Tom were ordered to submit

Courtesy Mrs. T. E. Gore

Dr. C. Van Zwalenburg and daughters

as evidence all agent Dias' letters written to Tom concerning the right-of-way purchases.[15]

The trial, which lasted three days and then reconvened on February 26th for the judge's decision, was a quiet one with almost no spectators. Hays, well dressed and clean shaven, sat between his lawyers. He denied that he had ever been the railroad's right-of-way agent, saying he had worked with it only to assist its entrance into Riverside. Four real estate agents, W. W. Wilson, Frank Tetley, J. Van de Grift, and B. B. Bush testified that Tom had organized a pool to buy right-of-way property. These agents were to secure property from the owners at a low price, then add on as high a "commission" as possible, and the sellers were to sign two receipts. One receipt was for the original price and the other included the "commissions" in a pool which went half to Tom and one-eighth each to the four real estate men.[16]

Some of the agents were reluctant to testify, especially Wilson who had a hard time remembering details. Mr. Bush, however, revealed all, as Tom had failed to pay the $2,000 which was due Bush on his sale to

15. *Los Angeles Times,* Feb. 14, 1906, and Federal Court Records.
16. *Riverside Enterprise,* Feb. 16, 1906.

the railroad of personally owned real estate. When Hays retained $2,000 of the $7,750 sale as his "commission," Bush said he began to suspect graft. He never got his $2,000. After this event Bush said that he had explained everything to W. M. Peck who was a lawyer for both the railroad and Mr. Bush.[17] Then Peck began his investigations which first revealed Tom's crookedness.

Under questioning, J. Ross Clark, the railroad's second vice-president,

B. B. Bush
As cartooned by Willard Cundiff

said that Tom requested that he be made their right-of-way agent. Hays would do it without commissions to aid the railroad and Riverside. Some land sellers testified in regard to the gross and net receipts that they had

17. *Riverside Enterprise*, Feb. 16, 1906.

signed. They said that they had been paid the lower figure by a check written by Tom. The trial closed on this note and the judge took ten days to reach a verdict. On February 26th Tom was convicted and ordered to pay $10,770 to the railroad. This included interest and court costs. Judge Wellborn, when he announced the verdict, was heard to mutter, "gross frauds . . . gross frauds." He also expressed amazement that the documents produced at this trial had not been available at the first. The books, however, were now owned by the Citizens Bank and their honest officers. Also the prosecuting attorneys during this trial had secured a court order that these records be produced. This had not been done previously.[18]

The *Riverside Daily Press* carried routine notice of the trial and Tom's conviction. The *Enterprise*, which had always been sympathetic to Tom, printed the details of the trial's beginning but failed to mention the verdict. The *Los Angeles Times* which had devoted little space to the trial announced the end with a headline, "A Verdict vs Debonair Tom for Sum Sought." It further commented that the trial had been little noticed by the public and that, "it was evident that the limelight has passed off Hays for good."[19]

18. *Los Angeles Times*, Feb. 27, 1906.
19. *Ibid.* A portion of this court case is missing in the Federal Record Center, Bell, Calif.

151

CHAPTER XVI

Riverside Acquires the Automobile and Motion Pictures but Loses Tom

An article headlined, "Tom Hays Figures in Divorce Case" appeared
in the June 14, 1906 *Press*, reprinted from the *Los Angeles Times*. Tom,
it seemed, was involved with an attractive Mrs. Warmington who was
one of the highlights of Ocean Park and Venice. Her husband, a Southern
Pacific Railroad engineer, was often away for long periods. According

Bordwell Photo

Street Parade 1904, *Main Street near Tenth, Orpheum Theatre right of electric pole*

to his wife he was unreasonably jealous of her friendship with Tom. She denied any wrongdoing, but wanted an immediate divorce. Hays, contrary to the previous comment of the *Times*, seemed to have difficulty keeping out of headlines.

At his home in Ocean Park with his wife and daughter Tom lived very well. He did a little real estate business and it was said that he had made money in some lucky deals. These together with the property and money inherited from his father-in-law kept his family comfortable. Also it was reputed that he collected over $50,000 when an English syndicate bought out the Aetna Oil Company of north Bakersfield.[1] As one of the original stockholders when it was incorporated in 1900 he had put considerable money into it. Presently he was looking at property for possible investment in the Malibu Hills where coal fields were rumored to exist. In the meantime many Riversiders were trying to untangle the string of problems Tom had left behind.

Mr. O. D. Wilhite said that he also had been flimflammed by debonair Tom Hays. Wilhite claimed he had just discovered that

1. *Riverside Daily Press*, Jan. 12, 1907.

cashier Tom previously had gotten him to sign a note for $1,500 when he owed the bank only $1,000.[2]

On June 14, 1906 Hays lost the rest of his Riverside property when U.S. Marshal H. Z. Osborne sold it at public auction on the Riverside

Orpheum Theatre

SIX NIGHTS
Commencing July 17

THE COX FAMILY
Chimes and Bell Quartette. The youngest and most famous quartette in America, introducing imitations of banjo chimes and church organ by use of the vocal chords.

MISS LILLIAN MELBOURNE
Chic Commedienne and Banjoist.

ASHER AND LEROY
Parisian Magicians in Comedy Magic.

LEE VICKERS
Black Face Entertainer.

MILDRED COX
The Clever Juvenile Singer and Dancer.

THE FUNNIEST OF ALL MOTION PICTURES
The Whole Dam Family and the Dam Dog; the Starting of the Great Ship Race Across the Atlantic.

The Latest of Illustrated Songs
"BUNKER HILL."

One show each night. Prices 20c and 25c. Matinee 10c. A $1.00 show for the smallest of prices.

Courthouse steps. The Salt Lake Railroad which had won the court case against him was unable to collect the $10,700 awarded and the court ordered the property sold. Tom's 12-acre orange grove was sold to E. H.

---

2. *Riverside Press and Horticulturist*, Dec. 31, 1906.

Courtesy Mrs. T. E. Gore *Dr. C. Van Zwalenburg's Waverly Electric Auto and family*

Rose which with the sale of some lots yielded the necessary funds to meet that judgment.

Two months later, on August 17th Superior Court Judge J. S. Noyes, who had played an uncertain role in Tom's affairs, resigned without warning. The news, which came from Los Angeles by telegram, was that his resignation was immediate. For some reason he decided not to complete his term which expired the following January. He had sold his recently built Main Street home and accepted a position with the Los Angeles law firm of Koefer and Bowers.[3] Some delay in court cases were caused by this resignation until his successor, Frank E. Densmore, was appointed. For four years Densmore had had a distinguished career as a Riverside lawyer serving with his half-brother, Lafayette Gill, in the firm of Gill and Densmore. Densmore was the outstanding choice of the local lawyers who knew of his 20 years of legal experience.

On September 20th a rather unusual situation occurred for a city the size of Riverside which then in 1906 had a population of almost 12,000 people. The jail stood empty with its door ajar. Was it because Tom was no longer in the city or was everyone busy roller skating? During this period the pastime became almost a craze. The Chemawa

---

3. *Riverside Daily Press*, Aug. 17, 1906.

Park pavilion, with a hardwood floor installed, became a popular place for the public to skate. In June, 1906 a new building called the Rubidoux Roller Rink opened at Market and Ninth streets. Owner-manager R. D. Lamar said that his large skating floor was full almost nightly although he charged 25 cents to skate and 10 cents to watch.[4]

Riverside Municipal Museum Collection   *The Robert Bettners with his mother*

Another amusement was that provided by the Orpheum Theater two blocks away in the old remodeled Skelley Building at 959 Main Street.[5] This may have been Riverside's first motion picture theater. On February 22, 1904 manager E. E. Lessenden staged the grand opening of this new movie house. Featured were Mable Martland, The Contortion Dancer; L. A. Toska, The Funny Tramp Juggler; and Essie Doreen, The London Drummer Girl Soubrette. Mr. Lessenden himself gave an illustrated song performance but the title of the opening movie was not mentioned. The theater advertised a daily matinee at 10 cents and two evening shows at 20 and 25 cents depending on the location of the seats.

Until the spring of 1906 this theater was a popular place. Every Monday it changed its motion picture. Early movies advertised were *Jack and the Beanstalk, The Whole Dam Family and the Dam Dog, The Martinique Disaster, Victims of the Storm* which was a Parisian picture in color, and *The Great Baltimore Fire.* On February 12, 1906

4. *Ibid*, June 18, 1906.
5. *Ibid*, Feb. 15, 1904.

the theater was still in operation showing a performance of *Everybody Works but Father*. It was competing, however, with Mme. Helena Modjeska who was appearing in *Mary Stuart* at the Loring Theatre. When this play was over the audience gave her an ovation but when Frank Miller wrapped her in a Polish flag made by a hotel guest it brought down the house.

Courtesy Albert Haight   *Box Springs Auto Race*

The Orpheum closed during the summers but for some reason in the fall of 1906 it did not reopen. Instead, another movie house, La Petite Theatre, at 753 Eighth Street, advertised as "Riverside's New Palace of Amusement," opened on November 17, 1906. By January, 1907 it had changd its name to the Palace of Pictures and announced any seat in the house cost 10 cents. By December 8th, however, it had some stiff competition. Another motion picture theater called The Auditorium opened in the new Patton Block opposite the courthouse. Showing colored motion pictures of the *Life of Christ* it was crowded every night.

Of even greater interest was the arrival in Riverside of the automobile. For those who could afford it and master the intricacies of driving, motoring became a diversion and often an obsession. Apparently the first automobile in Riverside arrived October 29, 1899. Its unexpected appearance that Sunday as it glided swiftly along Magnolia Avenue surprised the local residents. The touring car and its passengers were a part of Martin's Circus which had arrived in town. On Monday a colorful parade featured wild animals, sleek horses, many clowns, and carnival music played on the steam calliope. Bringing up the rear, and of great interest to the viewers, was the first automobile to appear on Main Street. The next mention of autos in the city was during the April, 1900 Street Fair when W. S. Collins' automobile and Dr. Sanborn's steam Locomotor from Redlands were in the Floral Parade.

Fortunately someone took the time to search out and write the story of the first ten cars owned by Riversiders. This account appeared in the September 23, 1902 issue of the *Press and Horticulturist*. From early 1900 to October, 1902 the ten cars added to the city's streets often scared the horses and their drivers. The first car was a Winton Touring bought by W. M. C. Jones in 1900. It did not prove too satisfactory as a year later he sold it and bought a new Winton which in 1902 was considered the fastest car in town. Next Hugh Bain, a wealthy retired mining engineer who lived at the Anchorage Hotel, appeared with a Locomobile Steam Rig. Then Orson T. Johnson, an early Riverside property owner, bought an Oldsmobile in Los Angeles and drove it home. Next Dr. C. Van Zwalenburg purchased his Waverly Electric and began to glide silently about the city on his medical visits. His daughter, Marian Gore, said that while he was first to order a car, delivery of that model was so slow others had theirs earlier.[6]

Next the Pequegnat brothers got an Oldsmobile. This was followed by Harry Kennedy's Toledo Steamer which occasionally had to stop for a bucket of water. Then the Riverside Bazaar Company bought two Oldsmobiles to use in their business. One was driven by A. W. Pequegnat who declared it was the most tried-and-true-tested of all the cars. Arthur Everest also acquired an Oldsmobile which completed the first ten cars purchased by Riversiders.

Local people not only bought cars, they also produced them.[7] A. W. Miller, who in 1901 had sold his planing mill to John Cresmer of San Jacinto, announced on September 20, 1902 that he was building a $20,000 brick auto factory on East Sixth Street near Eucalyptus Avenue. He had just placed an order for $4,000 worth of machinery which would be used in the manufacture of a new automobile to be called the Magnolia. He said that he already had six men working on the car's design. One employee was Watt Moreland who was an experienced mechanic.

---

6. Information Marian Gore, Jan. 1972.
7. Patterson. *Landmarks,* p. 107.

The factory, finished by January, 1903 produced its first car by May. A photograph of the single seated runabout and its factory appeared in the May 8, 1903 issue of the *Press and Horticulturist*. Floyd Followell, who said that he had a ride in the Magnolia automobile, declared it was a good car but that it could not compete with a Ford. The Magnolia sold for about $1,100 and a new Ford for $600. While reading electric light meters for the city James M. Wells said he had seen a Magnolia car in John Dougall's barn on West Eighth Street. Both Wells and Followell believe that about a dozen cars were produced in Riverside during the year the Magnolia Automobile Company stayed in business.[8]

According to the county assessor, by September, 1905 there were 31 automobiles owned in Riverside County. That year on Admission Day auto races were held at the Riverside Driving Track. The most interesting event featured Mrs. George Stanaham in her Autocar racing two other competitors. She came in second in the five mile race much to the enjoyment of the crowd.[9] On Thanksgiving, 1905, Ted Croosley of Riverside's Orange Valley Garage, promoted the first Riverside Box Springs auto race. The course was a dirt road from the top of the grade downhill to the Gage Canal crossing. To have raced uphill would have been impossible because the cars did not have enough power to go up without stopping to allow their engines to cool. George Bradbeer won the main event in a Premier with W. K. Cowan second in a Rambler.[10] The Southern California Auto Dealers Association sponsored the second yearly Thanksgiving Day race. This time 67 cars entered in seven classes and a big crowd turned out to watch. A six-cylinder Stevens-Duryea driven by Tommy Pillow, "a nervy little colored chauffeur" for A. B. Daniels of San Diego, won the big trophy.[11]

By 1906 automobiles could try a hill climb when the $19,600 four mile road on Mt. Rubidoux was completed by the Huntington Park Association. When the city failed to undertake the work, Frank Miller with Henry E. Huntington, C. Loring, C. Rumsey, A. S. White and many others organized the association to build the road and make a park on the mountain. On October 8th three sight-seeing tourists in their car were the first to make it to the top of Mt. Rubidoux. A week later Fred Twogood in his Oldsmobile also drove up and while he was there took the first photographs of the area.[12] Everyone who went up the new road to the top saw the clear, wonderful view of Riverside and the mountains beyond.

Frank Miller, convinced that the automobile would have an im-

8. Interview with James M. Wells and Floyd Followell, Nov., 1971.
9. *Riverside Daily Press*, Sept. 10, 1905.
10. *As You Find It*. Nov. 16, 1907.
11. *Ibid.*
12. *Riverside Daily Press*, Oct. 19, 1906.

portant place in California, built in the spring of 1906 on the corner of Market and Seventh streets his large Spanish-style Glenwood Mission Garage. Earlier he had gone east and inspected 21 different automobile

Courtesy James M. Wells   *Stearn's Pullman*

plants before buying his garage equipment and ten Stearns automobiles.[13] He charged people one dollar for a trip up and down the mountain and larger fees for longer trips. When the auto-ride business at the Glenwood was somewhat slow, Ed Miller, who was noted for his humor and amusing pranks, would play on the hotel chimes the tune "Come Away with Me Lucille, in My Merry Oldsmobile." Then hotel guests, reminded of the pleasures of motoring would go off for a spin enjoying "one hour's worth of exhilarating, refreshing, bumping, benzine buggy excitement". Another tune "Her Bright Smile Haunts Me Still" would be heard when a particularly attractive young lady would be making her departure. Sometimes when a solitary bell would ring out, townspeople would murmur that someone must have paid his bill.

Automobile driving at night became less hazardous when the city began in October, 1906 to install street lights first on Seventh, Eighth, and Ninth streets between Market and Orange and then later on Main Street between Fifth and Tenth streets. This was the first real effort to light the city.[14] Earlier George Frost and his Chamber of Commerce committee had worked with contractor S. L. Pillar and Frank Miller to design an attractive street light fixture. When finished it had an almost

13. *Ibid*, June 3, 1906.
14. *Ibid*, Oct. 30, 1906.

The new road to the top of Mt. Rubidoux

square cement pole topped by a triangle form having three small bell shaped lights and the double barred Indian Rain Cross. After the city accepted the design the Ornamental Stone Company of Riverside received the contract for their construction. Installation proceeded slowly and as late as 1912 they were being installed in the northwest section of town.

But what of Tom Hays? Nothing had been reported about him for six months. Winter had come to Riverside and the orange growers were out smudging to keep their fruit from freezing. The holidays ended the prosperous year of 1906 but ahead was 1907 with the country facing difficult business conditions and a panic on Wall Street. These things, however, would be of no concern to Tom.

On January 9, 1907 the news swept Riverside that he was seriously ill at his Ocean Park home. A week earlier he had developed a bad case of grippe and this turned into dropsy. His doctor was also concerned over possible heart trouble knowing that Tom had suffered much under the strain of the last three years. Soon he developed paralysis of the left side and only relatives and his lawyer friend, Earl Rogers, were permitted to visit him.

At the time of Tom's illness Frank Miller and his wife were preparing for their first trip to Europe. Miller had received a commission from President Roosevelt to build a hotel in the newly established Yosemite National Park. Visits to Norway, Denmark, Germany, and Switzerland were planned in order to look at Tyrolian type hotels.[16] There is, however, no record of Miller's ever building a hotel in Yosemite. Instead

11219. Cloister Tower,
Glenwood Mission Inn,
Riverside, Cal.

The Cloister Addition

in 1909 he began the Cloister addition to the Glenwood which was designed by his friend and architect Arthur B. Benton and which would occupy the northeast corner of the hotel block.

On July 29, 1911 the Mission Inn, as it was then called, issued a

16. *As You Find It*, Oct. 26, 1907.

small leaflet describing an elaborate dinner to mark the opening of this new Cloister addition which was described as follows: "Guests are cordially invited to inspect the recently completed $250,000 Cloister addition to the Mission Inn. The exterior is a copy of Carmel and San Gabriel Missions, examples of that unique American architecture which Fra Junipero Serra introduced, and which ended with his time. In the Cloister is a music room seating 500; great cathedral pipe organ made by the Kimball Company of Chicago; beautiful stained glass windows; a unique art room; and an interior cloistered walk with statues and paintings commemorating the period of the Mission Padres; a crypt banquet room; the private offices; and 50 new guest rooms.

"The 'Garden of the Bells' where hangs the famous Glenwood collection is well worth a visit. The San Juan Capistrano dome, rising above it, contains the echo organ. The roof of the Cloister is intended for amusements, among them tennis and roller-skating and the Carmel tower, surmounting it, will have a music studio and an observatory with a camera obscura and telescope, affording a view of the valley and mountains." In contrast to Tom's career Frank Miller's would be long and productive. All during his life he would add to his hotel and work to improve the city of Riverside.

As for Tom, he grew steadily worse. Headlines "End of Meteoric Career" appeared in the *Riverside Press*, January 12, 1907. Tom was dead. The paper printed a long review of his life pointing out that he was a 32nd degree Mason, a prominent Knights Templar, a member of the Riverside Foresters, Royal Arcanum, Woodman of the World, Knights of Pythias, Exalted Ruler of the Elks Club for two terms, President of the Chamber of Commerce for 1901 and 1902, and Chairman of the Riverside County Central Committee in 1900 and 1902. The article told of his life only in general terms, not referring to his bank and railroad difficulties. At the time of his death Hays was 39 years old. Surviving him were a mother in Pennsylvania, his wife Bertha, and a 16 year old daughter, Wanda, who later became a successful New York actress. The family remained comfortable with his $9,000 insurance, oil interests, and inherited wealth.

Tom's only known Riverside relatives were Mr. and Mrs. C. H. Cressman and daughter Marie. Charles Cressman, a cousin, came to Riverside from Philadelphia in 1892 with his wife, daughter, and mother-in-law Mary Hays.[17] For many years he was a deputy in the Riverside County Sheriff's office. In 1902 the family built a mission-style house, designed

17. *Riverside Reflex*, May 7, 1892.

by architects Burnham and Bleisner, on the northeast corner of Orange and Fourth streets. A little later these same architects designed Tom's bungalow. The Hays and Cressman families were always friendly.

The *Riverside Enterprise*, a newspaper always sympathetic to Hays, told the story of his death a little differently than the *Press*. With headlines of "Death Claims Sufferer" the article explained how he went down to the grave cheerful to the last, keeping his troubles to himself. By doing this his doctor believed that Tom had hardened his heart muscles, causing death due to "myocarditis—a form of broken heart." Earl Rogers declared this was true saying that Tom, all through his troubles and court trials, kept his optimistic spirit. Rogers, who was at Tom's bedside when he died, called him an important man and a born leader of Riverside. He said that with the death of Tom Hays an outstanding citizen of southern California was gone.[18]

---

18. *Riverside Enterprise*, Jan. 12, 1907.

THE AUTHOR

Esther Klotz, except for various periods spent in Europe, has lived most of her life in Riverside County. Born in Hemet, she is a graduate of that city's high school, the Riverside City College, and the University of California at Berkeley. As both her maternal and paternal grandparents came to southern California in the boom of 1887 she has always been interested in the area's local history, collecting its books and material.

During the last few years she has worked chiefly with the Riverside Museum Associates and the Riverside Cultural Heritage Board serving as the latter's first chairman. Presently she is chairman of the "Friends of the Mission Inn" and a member of the Riverside Pioneer Historical Society, the Orange County Historical Society and the Historical Society of Southern California. She lives in Riverside with her husband, Dr. Leo J. Klotz, a plant pathologist at the University of California, Riverside.

The text for this book is set in Electra and printed on Warren's lustro enamel dull paper. Most of the decorative chapter headings are from *The Land of Sunshine Fruit and Flowers*. Columbus, Ohio: Ward Brothers, 1898 in the author's collection.

BIBLIOGRAPHY

Benton, Arthur B. *The Mission Inn.* Los Angeles: Segnogram Publishing Co., 1907.

Brown, John, Jr., and James Boyd. *History of San Bernardino and Riverside Counties.* Chicago: Western Historical Assn., Lewis Publishing Co., 1922. 3 vols.

Cohn, Alfred and Joe Chisholm. *Take the Witness.* New York: F. A. Stokes Co., 1934.

Coop, L. G. *Who's Who in Riverside: A Book of Cartoons by Willard Cundiff.* Los Angeles: Thorpe Engineering Co., 1908.

Gale, Zona. *Frank Miller of the Mission Inn.* New York: D. Appleton-Century, 1938.

Guinn, James M. *Historical and Biographical Record of Southern California.* Chicago: Chapman Publishing Co., 1902.

——————. *A History of California and an Extended History of its Southern Coast Counties.* Los Angeles: Historic Record Co., 1907. 2 vols.

Holmes, Elmer W. *A History of Riverside County.* Los Angeles: Historic Record Co., 1912.

History of Southern California: Pen Pictures of the Garden of the World. Chicago: Lewis Publishing Co., 1890.

Johnson, William A. *Through the Years: A Family Album.* n. p. 1955.

Klotz, Esther H., Harry W. Lawton and Joan H. Hall, eds. *A History of Citrus in the Riverside Area.* Riverside: Riverside Museum Press, 1969.

Patterson, Tom. *Landmarks of Riverside.* Riverside: Press-Enterprise Co., 1964.

Robinson, W. W. *Lawyers of Los Angeles: A History of the Los Angeles Bar Association and of the Bar of Los Angeles County.* Los Angeles: Ward Ritchie Press, 1959.

Rodman, Willoughby. *History of the Bench and Bar of Southern California.* Los Angeles: W. J. Porter, 1909.

St. Johns, Adela Rogers. *Final Verdict.* New York: Doubleday and Co., 1962.

Swett, Ira L. *The Riverside and Arlington Electric Railway.* Los Angeles: Ira L. Swett Co., 1962.

Wolfe, W. C., ed. *Men of California.* San Francisco: Pacific Art Co., 1901.

Tigner, J. H. *Souvenir of the City of Riverside.* Los Angeles: Riverside Fire Department, Tigner Publishing Co., 1906.

DOCUMENTS, PAMPHLETS, MANUSCRIPTS, ARTICLES, and NEWSPAPERS

Articles from *As You Find It*. Riverside Magazine, 1907-1908.

Chase, E. A. *Notebooks*. In the Riverside Public Library, 1916-1918. 12 vols.

Estudillo, Miguel. *Papers and Notebooks*. Bancroft Library.

Haglund, R. L. *Chronology, History of Riverside Banking*. Riverside: Security First National Bank, 1966.

Klotz, Esther H. "Pomona's Palomares Hotel." *Pomona Valley Historian*, January 1970.

Klotz, Esther H., Harry W. Lawton, and Joan H. Hall, eds. *Reports*. Riverside Museum Association (quarterly), 1964-1968.

Lawton, Harry W. "Riverside's Pioneer Chinese." Riverside: *Press-Enterprise*. Five newspaper articles, February 8-12, 1959.

Los Angeles Federal Record Center. Criminal Cases: United States vs. H. T. Hays (case No. 1956), and San Pedro, Los Angeles, and Salt Lake Railway vs. H. T. Hays (case No. 1093). Bell, California.

Riverside California: Home of the Orange. Los Angeles: Ledger Publishing Co., n. d. Ca. 1893.

Riverside: The Home of the Orange. Los Angeles: The Sun Drug Co., n. d. Ca. 1903.

Picturesque Riverside. Riverside Press Printing, n. d. Ca. 1904.

New Year's Annual. Riverside Daily Press, 1898.

Riverside Polo Club *Minutes*, 1892. Collection Riverside Municipal Museum.

Riverside County Board of Supervisors *Minutes*.

Riverside County Courthouse Deed Records.

Riverside City Council *Minutes*.

Riverside County Clerk's Records.

Riverside City *Directories*. 1889-1907.

Riverside Daily Press.

Riverside Press and Horticulturist.

Riverside Reflex.

The Phoenix.

Riverside Enterprise.

The Los Angeles Times.

ACKNOWLEDGMENTS

It is obvious to the reader that almost all of the material used in the preparation of this book came from the Riverside and Los Angeles newspapers. For this reason the author has greatly appreciated the facilities of the Riverside Public Library and the helpfulness of its staff. Riverside is very fortunate that its old newspapers, almost complete, are on microfilm and readily accessible. Librarians Dorothy F. Smith and Zoma Henry of this institution over the past five years have been especially helpful with their expert assistance.

The author is also grateful for information and materials supplied by other libraries. These are the Huntington, San Marino; the Bancroft, University of California, Berkeley; the Southwest Museum, Los Angeles; the Los Angeles Public Library; the Sherman Foundation, Corona del Mar; and the Los Angeles Federal Records Center, Bell. The Bancroft with its rare issues of the *Riverside Reflex* and large collection of early Riverside ephemera was invaluable. There at the suggestion of Tom Patterson, the author read the Miguel Estudillo papers pertaining to the Hays case. The Los Angeles Public and the Sherman Foundation Libraries provided back issues of the *Los Angeles Times* which described in detail the court trials. Dr. William Hendricks, director and Edwin W. Tomlinson, librarian at the attractive Sherman Foundation assisted in locating other useful matter.

Throughout the text, in the footnotes, and picture captions information and materials from many people and institutions are acknowledged unless supplied from the author's collection. Other helpful people are Marian Webster who has furnished unique material, Mr. and Mrs. Gordon Pattee (deceased) who graciously showed the Tom Hays house then owned by them, Mrs. Donald Fullerton (deceased) daughter of Robert Bettner, and Mrs. M. L. Castleman who supplied news clippings. Riverside County Clerk Donald D. Sullivan kindly found some old court cases of value. To all of these people the author expresses appreciation for their kind assistance.

Many of the valuable old photographs and some source material are from the Riverside Municipal Museum. The author is sincerely grateful for the use of these and the helpfulness of the museum staff, especially